WORLD WAR II

VISUAL ENCYCLOPEDIA

Senior Editor Fleur Star
Senior Art Editor Stefan Podhorodecki
Extra editorial assistance Francesca Baines, Caroline Bingham,
Charlie Galbraith, Chris Hawkes, Simon Mumford, Victoria Pyke, Jenny Sich
Extra illustration Stefan Podhorodecki, Jemma Westing
Managing Editor Linda Esposito
Managing Art Editor Philip Letsu
Jackets Assistant Claire Gell
Jacket Designer Mark Cavanagh
Jacket Development Manager Sophia M Tampakopoulos Turner
Picture Researchers Sarah Smithies and Sarah Ross
Producer, Pre-production Francesca Wardell
Senior Producer Gemma Sharpe

Publisher Andrew Macintyre
Associate Publishing Director Liz Wheeler
Publishing Director Jonathan Metcalf

Designed, edited and project-managed for DK by Dynamo Ltd.

Written by Brian Williams
Consultant: Reg Grant

First published in Great Britain in 2015 by
Dorling Kindersley Limited,
80 Strand, London WC2R 0RL

Copyright © 2015 Dorling Kindersley Limited
A Penguin Random House Company

10 9 8 7 6
022–282969–June/15

A CIP catalogue record for this book
is available from the British Library.

ISBN: 978-0-2412-0699-7

Printed and bound in UAE

A WORLD OF IDEAS:
SEE ALL THERE IS TO KNOW

www.dk.com

CONTENTS

CHAPTER ONE: KEY PLAYERS

CHAPTER TWO: MILITARY PERSONNEL

CHAPTER THREE: KEY EVENTS & BATTLES

CHAPTER FOUR: TECHNOLOGY OF WAR

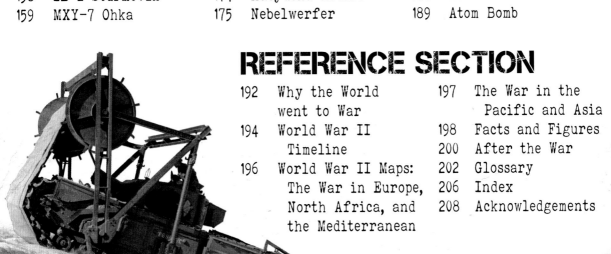

REFERENCE SECTION

CHAPTER ONE:
KEY PLAYERS

World War II (1939–1945) was fought by the Axis powers (Germany, Italy, and Japan) against the Allies (led by Britain, the US, and the USSR). Fighting began in 1939 when Germany attacked Poland, and spread across the globe. Millions of people were caught up in the conflict, but the course of the war was shaped by a handful of key individuals – charismatic leaders, military heroes, and those fighting the horrors of the Holocaust.

"Men must not sleep; they ought to know that a thunderstorm is coming up."

Adolf Hitler
speech in Munich, 20 April 1933

LEADERS OF NATIONS

Wartime leaders had to make hard decisions and take decisive action. This meant sharing plans with allies, but in practice they often kept secrets from one another. Decisions made by the great war leaders determined the fates of millions of people around the world.

ADOLF HITLER

Leading the Nazi Party, Hitler took power in Germany in 1933, crushing all opposition. He dreamed of a German "super race". He wanted to create a new empire (Third Reich), and destroy European Jews and Communism. His attack on Poland in 1939 started WWII.

❝ ... people will more easily fall victims to a big lie than to a small one. ❞

LEADERSHIP STYLE

Hitler made long, passionate speeches to rally supporters and mock enemies. Always sure that he was right, he told generals how to fight their battles. When Germany started losing, he became a recluse, commanding from a bunker under Berlin, but refused to surrender.

The leader
Hitler fought in WWI and felt Germany had been humiliated in defeat. He made it his mission to make Germany strong again and avenge their defeat. In 1934, he declared himself *Führer* (leader), ruling as a dictator.

KEY DATES

1889: Born 20 April, in Austria.

1918: Awarded Iron Cross (WWI).

1921: Head of Nazi Party (German Workers' Party).

1933: Takes power.

1944: Escaped assassination plot in July.

1945: Died 30 April; shot himself in Berlin bunker.

JOSEPH STALIN

Stalin ruthlessly removed all rivals to rule the Soviet Union. He took part in the Russian Revolution in 1917, and became a Communist dictator after Lenin died. In 1939, Stalin signed a "no-war" pact with Hitler. However, he joined the Allies in 1941, after Hitler invaded Russia.

LEADERSHIP STYLE

Stalin killed opponents in the Communist Party and the army in a series of "purges". Millions died in prison camps or were executed by Stalin's secret police. In 1941, he made himself supreme commander of the Red Army, but seldom visited battlefields or war-hit cities.

> **" A single death is a tragedy: a million deaths is a statistic. "**

KEY DATES

1878: Born 18 December.

1917: Joined Russian Revolution.

1924: Followed Lenin as Soviet leader.

1935: Began to purge enemies and rivals.

1939: Agreed a pact with Hitler to divide Poland.

1941: Joined Allies after Hitler attacked Russia.

1945: Ordered Communists to seize power in eastern Europe.

1953: Died 5 March.

Man of steel
Stalin means "man of steel". His real name was Iosif Vissarionovich Dzhugashvili. Allied leaders Churchill and Roosevelt found him suspicious and secretive. The Soviet dictator had his own plans – for a post-war Europe dominated by Communism.

WINSTON CHURCHILL

Churchill was an inspirational leader as Britain's prime minister (1940-1945). After an adventurous life as a soldier, war reporter, and politician, many people thought Churchill was "past it" when he became war leader in 1940.

> **We shall defend our island, whatever the cost may be... we shall never surrender.**

LEADERSHIP STYLE

Churchill was famed for his stirring wartime speeches. He was known for his "V for Victory" hand sign, his energy and mood-swings, and his wish to run everything. He had to be prevented from joining the D-Day landings.

KEY DATES

1874: Born 30 November.

1900: Member of Parliament until 1964.

1911-1915: Navy minister.

1929-1939: Out of government. Warns of Nazi danger.

1940: British prime minister, led war effort.

1945: Lost general election.

1951: Prime minister until 1955.

1965: Died 24 January.

United leaders
Allied leaders Churchill, Roosevelt, and Stalin met at Yalta (Crimea) in 1945 to plan the final defeat of Germany. Soon afterwards, Churchill lost power in Britain's election. This amazed Stalin. There were no free elections in the Communist USSR.

BENITO MUSSOLINI

Benito Mussolini took Italy to war in 1940. Known as Il Duce ("The Leader"), he served in the army during WWI, and later founded Italy's Fascist Party. Mussolini was prime minister from 1922 before he began ruling as a dictator.

LEADERSHIP STYLE

Mussolini wore military uniform and gave fiery speeches. He dreamed of an Italian empire, and called the Mediterranean "our sea". His black-shirt Fascists inspired the German Nazis, but Hitler thought Mussolini was weak.

&& For my part I prefer fifty thousand rifles to five million votes. 99

KEY DATES

- **1883:** Born 29 July.
- **1926:** Ruled Italy as dictator.
- **1935:** Invaded Ethiopia.
- **1938:** Became Hitler's ally.
- **1940:** Invaded Greece.
- **1943:** Arrested after Allies invaded Italy; rescued by German commandos.
- **1945:** Recaptured, shot by Italian partisans. Died 28 April.

Italian ambition
Il Duce wanted to modernize Italy by improving roads and railways. He hoped joining Hitler would boost Italy's power in the Mediterranean, and gain colonies in Africa.

EMPEROR HIROHITO

Hirohito was Japan's emperor from 1926. The country was moving to democracy, but instead the army took charge. Hirohito did not support Japan's march to war, but could do little to prevent it. In 1945, knowing his country faced destruction, he urged the government to surrender.

> **❝ The fruits of victory are tumbling into our mouth too quickly. ❞**

LEADERSHIP STYLE

The emperor was rarely seen in public and many Japanese considered him to be a god. His leadership style was formal, and his behaviour was shaped by traditional codes of honour.

● KEY DATES

1901: Born 29 April, son of Emperor Yoshihito.

1921: Visited England, which he liked for its more casual ways.

1926: Became Japanese emperor after his father died.

1941: Japan at war with the US and other Allies.

1945: Remained as emperor as post-war Japan modernized.

1989: Died 7 January.

A private man
Photographs of Hirohito with his family were seen only after the war, when Japanese society began to change. Quiet and studious, he was criticized for not stopping the war party who took over the Japanese government.

CHIANG KAI-SHEK

Chiang, also known as Jiang Jieshi, led the Chinese Nationalist government, fighting the Japanese and the Chinese Communists led by Mao Zedong. In 1941, Chiang joined the top Allied leaders after China declared war on Germany. He was boosted by aid from the US.

> **&& Mao has a soft-as-cotton outer layer, with sharp needles hidden inside... 99**

LEADERSHIP STYLE

After military college, Chiang supported the new Chinese Republic formed in 1912, but from the 1920s, he ruled more or less as a dictator. During the fighting in China, millions suffered and lost their lives.

KEY DATES

1887: Born 31 October.

1925: Led the Kuomintang (Chinese Nationalist Party), after death of president Sun Yat-sen.

1927: Began fighting Chinese Communists.

1937: Led fight against Japanese invasion.

1949: Exiled to Formosa (Taiwan).

1975: Died 5 April.

High hopes
The Allies hoped that Chiang would lead China to democracy. But China's civil war resumed after Japan's defeat. By 1949, the Nationalists had lost to Mao's Communists. Chiang ruled only over Formosa (Taiwan).

MAO ZEDONG

Mao Zedong led the Chinese Communist Party. He fought two successful guerrilla wars, one in the 1930s against the Chinese Nationalists, and the other against the invading Japanese (1937–1945). By 1945, Mao had much of China under Communist control.

LEADERSHIP STYLE

Mao was an organizer. He formed the Communists into a disciplined army who obeyed orders and were ready to die for the cause. He gained support from the USSR, while his rival Chiang Kai-Shek was backed by the US.

66 The people are the sea that the revolutionary swims in... 99

KEY DATES

1893: Born 26 December.

1921: Helped found the Chinese Communist Party.

1927: At war with the Nationalist Kuomintang.

1934: Led the "Long March" of Communists to escape Nationalists.

1937: Joined Chiang Kai-Shek to fight Japan.

1945: Civil war resumed after Japan's defeat.

1949: Leader of Communist China.

 1976: Died 9 September.

Strength in numbers
Mao swelled the Chinese People's Army from 50,000 to 500,000. He believed China's millions of poor peasants could defeat the Japanese and become an army that would change Chinese society.

FRANKLIN ROOSEVELT

Franklin Roosevelt was US president for more than 12 years. At first, many Americans wanted to keep out of the war, but after Japan attacked the US in 1941, public opinion changed. Roosevelt ordered US forces into battle against Japan and Germany.

> **" A date which will live in infamy. "**
> 7 December 1941, Japan attacks Pearl Harbor

LEADERSHIP STYLE

Roosevelt travelled overseas to plan war strategy with battlefield commanders and Allied leaders Churchill and Stalin. The radio talks that Roosevelt broadcast to Americans greatly increased his popularity.

Allies unite
Roosevelt suggested the name "United Nations" for the countries fighting against Germany, Italy, and Japan. The president died just a month after meeting Allied leaders at the Yalta conference in 1945.

KEY DATES

 1882: Born 30 January.

 1921: Contracted polio; learned to walk again.

1933: President of the US.

1941: Declared war on Japan after Pearl Harbor.

1944: Started unique fourth term as president.

 1945: Died 12 April.

HARRY TRUMAN

Truman took over as president of the United States when Franklin Roosevelt died suddenly on 12 April 1945. Truman faced enormous decisions. The most difficult was ordering atomic bombs to be dropped on Japan to end the war.

LEADERSHIP STYLE

With little experience of world affairs, Truman relied on advisers as he met other Allied leaders to reshape the post-war world. He had a reputation for speaking his mind. Truman presided over the rebuilding of Japan and Europe, and the new "cold war" with the USSR.

❝ The responsibility of great states is to serve and not to dominate the world. ❞

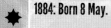 **KEY DATES**

- **1884:** Born 8 May.
- **1917:** Served in US Army in WWI.
- **1934:** US senator.
- **1944:** Roosevelt's vice-president.
- **1945:** President of the US.
- **1948–1952:** Served full term as president.
- **1972:** Died 26 December.

Peacekeeper
Truman oversaw the creation of the new United Nations (founded 24 October 1945) to maintain world peace, as well as the 1949 founding of NATO (North Atlantic Treaty Organization). His government helped to rebuild war-torn Europe.

MILITARY COMMANDERS

World War II commanders led the biggest armies, navies, and air forces ever sent into battle. They had to follow government orders while also planning battle strategies – and keep up the spirits of their troops, try to supply them with enough weapons, kit, food, fuel, and ammunition, and out-guess the enemy. For every battle, a commander had to plan for victory, but also prepare for defeat.

ERWIN ROMMEL

General Rommel, known as "The Desert Fox", was a German who was both respected and feared by enemies. His Afrika Korps won key battles in the Desert War in North Africa until their defeat by Britain's General Montgomery. By 1943, Rommel had been driven out of North Africa.

LEADERSHIP STYLE

Rommel was outstanding as a tank commander. His secret was to use surprise and speed. After his defeat in North Africa, he was ordered to defend France against Allied invasion, but failed to stop the D-Day landings. Wounded in an air attack, Rommel took no further part in the D-Day battles.

❝ Be an example to your men, in your duty and in private life. ❞

KEY DATES

1891: Born 15 November.

1912: Joined German Army, served in WWI and WWII.

1940: Panzer commander in France and Belgium.

1941–1943: Led in North Africa.

1944: Injured in France.

1944: Died 14 October.

Death sentence
Rommel was accused of plotting to kill Hitler. Because of his fame and service in North Africa, Rommel was allowed to commit suicide instead of being executed.

19

HERMANN GOERING

In 1940, as commander of the German air force (Luftwaffe), Goering promised Hitler that his aircraft could defeat Britain. However, the Luftwaffe failed to win the Battle of Britain. Then, after 1941, it failed to save German forces from being beaten in Russia. By 1944, the Allies had command of the air.

> 66 **Would you rather have butter or guns? Guns will make us strong, butter will only make us fat.** 99

LEADERSHIP STYLE

Goering loved to strut about in a fancy marshal's uniform decorated with medals. A fighter pilot in World War I, he expected too much from the Luftwaffe and was slow to use new German technology (such as the V-2 rocket and jet fighters). By 1944, Hitler no longer believed Goering's boasts.

KEY DATES

 1893: Born 12 January.

1915–1918: WWI pilot.

1922: Joined the Nazi Party.

1945: Charged with war crimes.

 1946: Died 15 October; killed himself with poison.

Hitler's adviser
Goering joined the Nazi Party in 1922, becoming one of Hitler's closest government advisers. When his Luftwaffe failed to win Hitler victory, Goering lost face. After the war he was convicted of war crimes, but killed himself just before he was due to be hanged.

ARTHUR HARRIS

Air Marshal Harris led the British Royal Air Force's Bomber Command. Nicknamed "Bomber Harris", he believed that bombing German cities would destroy factory production and the enemy's will to fight. However, his crews suffered heavy losses.

LEADERSHIP STYLE

Harris was criticized for attacking civilians rather than military targets, but stuck to his strategy. He thought massive raids would bring victory. Raids on Hamburg in 1943 killed more than 40,000 people, while the fire-bombing of Dresden in 1945 left 25,000 people dead.

> **❝ They (the Nazis) sowed the wind and now they are going to reap the whirlwind. ❞**

KEY DATES

1892: Born 13 April.

1918–1946: Served in the British Royal Air Force.

1942–1945: Commander of British bombers attacking Germany.

1984: Died 5 April.

Unrewarded
The bombing raids Harris ordered were controversial, even at the time. After the war, Harris retired without the full honours given to other commanders.

ISOROKU YAMAMOTO

After fighting in the Russo-Japanese war (1904–1905), Admiral Yamamoto rose to command the 1st Fleet in 1939. Then, in 1941, he masterminded Japan's attack on the US naval base at Pearl Harbor. The attack made Yamamoto famous, but he feared the might of the US response.

66 The fiercest serpent may be overcome by a swarm of ants. 99

LEADERSHIP STYLE

Yamamoto was a careful planner. As navy chief, he favoured aircraft over battleships. He chose aircraft carriers to launch attack planes on the US Pacific Fleet. But the US broke Japanese secret codes. This won them the Battle of Midway, and destroyed Yamamoto's Pacific strategy.

KEY DATES

 1884: Born 4 April.

1904: Served in the Imperial Japanese Navy.

1939: Commanded the Japanese navy.

 1943: Died 18 April, when his plane was shot down by Allied fighters.

Hungry for victory
After Pearl Harbor, Yamamoto hoped for one more decisive victory over the US Navy. He knew Japan would lose in a long war.

CHESTER NIMITZ

Admiral Nimitz commanded all US naval forces in the Pacific. His task was to rebuild the Pacific Fleet after the attack on Pearl Harbor in December 1941. Under his leadership, the Fleet won important battles against the Japanese navy. Nimitz signed the peace agreement with Japan in 1945.

LEADERSHIP STYLE

Nimitz helped plan the Allied strategy of "island hopping". Key Japanese islands were captured one by one, using ships, planes, and troops. With the restored Pacific Fleet, Nimitz had more power to call on than any other naval commander in history.

> **&& Leadership consists of picking good men and helping them do their best. 99**

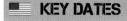
KEY DATES

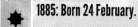

1885: Born 24 February.

1905: Joined US Navy, served throughout WWI and WWII.

1941–1945: Commander of US Pacific Fleet.

1966: Died 20 February.

Big mistakes
Nimitz said that the Japanese made three of the biggest mistakes an attack force ever could at Pearl Harbor. They struck on a Sunday, when many sailors were off-base; they missed the docks; and they missed the oil tanks.

DOUGLAS MACARTHUR

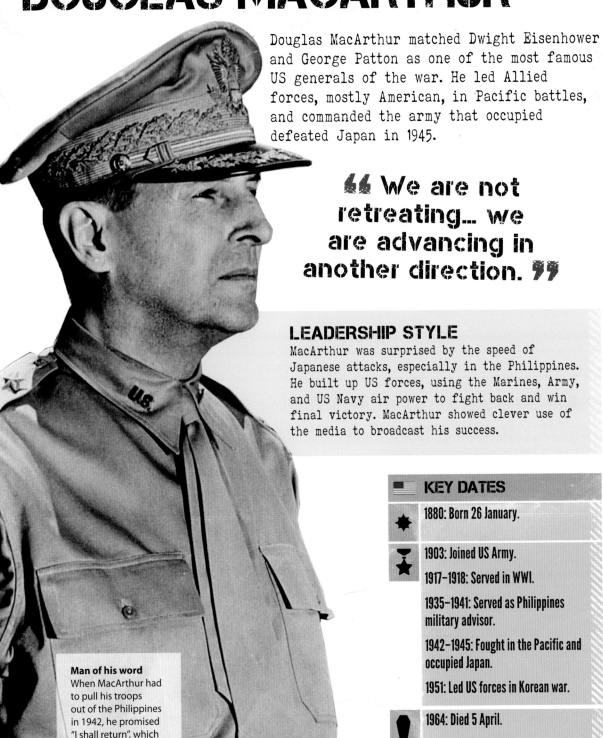

Douglas MacArthur matched Dwight Eisenhower and George Patton as one of the most famous US generals of the war. He led Allied forces, mostly American, in Pacific battles, and commanded the army that occupied defeated Japan in 1945.

> **❝ We are not retreating... we are advancing in another direction. ❞**

LEADERSHIP STYLE

MacArthur was surprised by the speed of Japanese attacks, especially in the Philippines. He built up US forces, using the Marines, Army, and US Navy air power to fight back and win final victory. MacArthur showed clever use of the media to broadcast his success.

KEY DATES

1880: Born 26 January.

1903: Joined US Army.

1917–1918: Served in WWI.

1935–1941: Served as Philippines military advisor.

1942–1945: Fought in the Pacific and occupied Japan.

1951: Led US forces in Korean war.

1964: Died 5 April.

Man of his word
When MacArthur had to pull his troops out of the Philippines in 1942, he promised "I shall return", which he did in 1944.

TOMOYUKI YAMASHITA

Tomoyuki Yamashita led Japan's invasion of Malaya, 1941–1942. He took the surrender of Singapore, the British fortress island, in February 1942. His Japanese troops fought in the Philippines, including the battles for Bataan and Corregidor.

LEADERSHIP STYLE

Japan's army and navy controlled the country's government. But generals were often rivals, and commanders sometimes ignored Yamashita's orders. His fast-moving campaign in Malaya took the Allies by surprise. He'd learned modern warfare methods in Germany, and short-cut his way around old-fashioned defences.

❝ I believe that I have tried my best for my army. ❞

KEY DATES

1885: Born 8 November.

1906–1945: Served in Japanese Army. Battle zones fought in included:
1937–1939: China
1939: Manchuria
1941–1942: Malaya and Singapore
1944–1945: Philippines

1946: Died 23 February, hanged for war crimes.

Fallen general
Yamashita was called "The Tiger of Malaya" for his victories. As general in charge, he paid the penalty for the actions of his soldiers. He was found guilty of war crimes in the Philippines.

GEORGI ZHUKOV

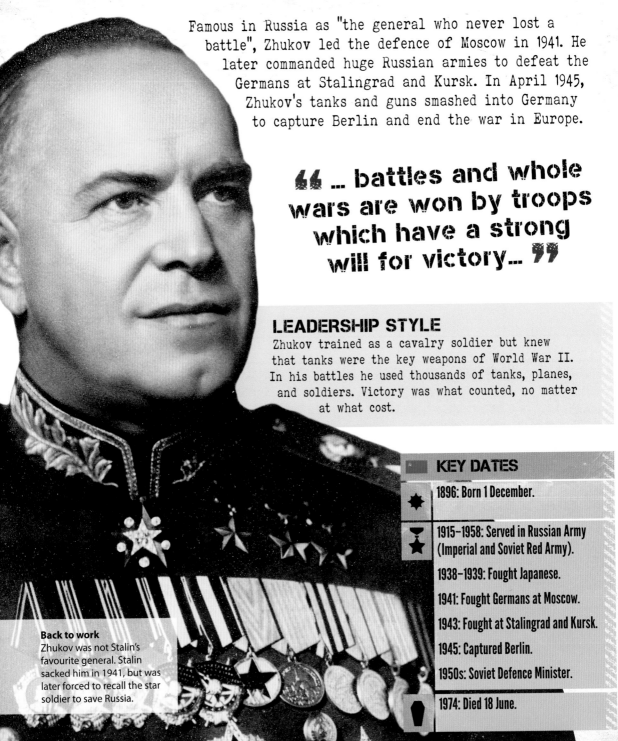

Famous in Russia as "the general who never lost a battle", Zhukov led the defence of Moscow in 1941. He later commanded huge Russian armies to defeat the Germans at Stalingrad and Kursk. In April 1945, Zhukov's tanks and guns smashed into Germany to capture Berlin and end the war in Europe.

66 ... battles and whole wars are won by troops which have a strong will for victory... 99

LEADERSHIP STYLE

Zhukov trained as a cavalry soldier but knew that tanks were the key weapons of World War II. In his battles he used thousands of tanks, planes, and soldiers. Victory was what counted, no matter at what cost.

KEY DATES

1896: Born 1 December.

1915–1958: Served in Russian Army (Imperial and Soviet Red Army).

1938–1939: Fought Japanese.

1941: Fought Germans at Moscow.

1943: Fought at Stalingrad and Kursk.

1945: Captured Berlin.

1950s: Soviet Defence Minister.

1974: Died 18 June.

Back to work
Zhukov was not Stalin's favourite general. Stalin sacked him in 1941, but was later forced to recall the star soldier to save Russia.

HEINZ GUDERIAN

A skilful battlefield commander, Guderian led German tank armies into Poland, France, and Russia. He sent in tanks and infantry, backed by planes and artillery, for fast-moving attacks. This blitzkrieg ("lightning war") was the secret of Germany's success from 1939 to 1941.

LEADERSHIP STYLE

Guderian's panzers (armoured units) raced to surprise the enemy. Tanks led the charge of armoured vehicles, with infantry tucked in behind, and artillery at the rear. His status suffered when German tanks lost the Battle of Kursk (in Russia) in 1943.

❝ If the tanks succeed then victory follows. ❞

KEY DATES

1888: Born 17 June.

1907–1945: Served in German Army, commanded tanks. Battle zones included Poland 1939; France 1940; Russia 1941–1943; western Europe 1944.

1945–1948: Prisoner of war.

1954: Died 14 May.

Tank commander
Heinz Guderian often argued with Hitler, and was sacked after losing the Battle of Kursk. He was later restored to command but, by 1944, Guderian knew Germany was beaten.

DWIGHT EISENHOWER

Eisenhower became the best-known general of World War II. The genial American commanded US forces in Europe from 1942 and oversaw Allied landings in North Africa. As supreme commander on 5 June 1944, "Ike" decided to risk poor weather and order the D-Day invasion of France: "Ok, let's go."

❝ The hopes and prayers of liberty-loving people everywhere march with you... ❞

LEADERSHIP STYLE

Eisenhower's chief skill was in planning. His diplomacy helped smooth tensions between leaders, but some critics thought he was too cautious.

Commanding leader
Eisenhower returned to the US as a national hero. He left the army in 1952, then served as US President 1953–1961.

KEY DATES

1890: Born 14 October.

1915–1952: US Army.

1942: Led US forces in Europe. Commanded Allied landings in North Africa.

1944: Supreme Commander, D-Day.

US president: 1953–1961

1969: Died 28 March.

BERNARD MONTGOMERY

"Monty" was Britain's most successful World War II general. He restored confidence to Allied troops in North Africa after defeats by Rommel. In 1944, he commanded Allied ground forces in the D-Day landings. In May 1945, Monty took the German Army's surrender in northern Germany.

LEADERSHIP STYLE

Montgomery was known for the beret he often wore. He spoke clearly and precisely. His air of self-belief inspired others, but did not always make him popular with other generals.

> ❝ If we lose the war in the air we lose the war and we lose it quickly. ❞

⬭ KEY DATES

1887: Born 17 November.

1908: Joined British Army.

1942: Commander of Allied forces in Egypt, winning victory at the Battle of El Alamein (November 1942).

1951–1958: Deputy supreme commander of NATO forces in Europe.

1976: Died 24 March.

General Monty
Monty believed in careful planning and huge strength to ensure victory. After the war he became deputy supreme commander of NATO forces in Europe.

EXTRAORDINARY FIGHTERS

World War II produced many heroes from many nations. They were people of extraordinary courage and endurance who were often willing to risk – and give – their lives to save others. They acted out of anger, excitement, fear, and determination in the terrible confusion of battle and performed feats of outstanding bravery that won them medals in recognition of their special contribution.

DOUGLAS BADER

Bader lost both legs in a pre-war flying accident, but rejoined the British Royal Air Force as a fighter pilot when WWII began. In the Battle of Britain he led a squadron of Canadian pilots. Later, he commanded a large battle group of fighters to attack raiding German bombers.

66 If you came out of the Sun, the enemy could not see you. 99

WHY A HERO?
Bader walked on artificial legs. In 1941, his Spitfire collided with a German plane. He managed to escape by parachute, but lost one of the legs. Bader was held as a prisoner of war, and the RAF dropped him a new leg by parachute.

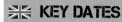 **KEY DATES**

 1910: Born 21 February.

 1931: Crashed and lost both his legs.

1939: Rejoined RAF as a fighter pilot.

1940: Fought in Battle of Britain.

1941–1945: Prisoner of war in Germany.

1982: Died 5 September.

50/50
Bader claimed to have shot down 30 enemy planes. However, his official "score" was 22.5. When two pilots claimed to have shot down the same enemy aircraft, they got half each!

JAMES NICOLSON

James Brindley Nicolson was 23 in 1940, when he fought in the Battle of Britain. He won the only Victoria Cross medal awarded to a pilot. Although wounded, and with his plane on fire, he managed to shoot down an enemy aircraft.

> **❝ The purpose of a fighter pilot is to shoot down the enemy... ❞**

WHY A HERO?

Nicolson was in a "dogfight" (close combat with another aircraft) over southern England when a Me-110 fighter plane set his Hurricane on fire. Badly burned, he struggled to dive, attack, and shoot down another German raider before bailing out. He parachuted to the ground, where a Home Guard soldier shot at him, mistaking him for a German!

Did not see peace
Nicolson went back to flying with the RAF, but was killed in an air crash in the Bay of Bengal in May 1945.

KEY DATES

1917: Born 29 April.

1936: Joined RAF.

1940: Awarded Victoria Cross.

1941: Returned to flying.

1943: Led fighter squadron in Burma.

1945: Died in a plane crash, 2 May.

NADYA POPOVA

Nadezhda ("Nadya") Popova flew with the "Night Witches" as one of the Soviet Union's female pilots. The Germans gave her group its name because they "whooshed" to attack at night, often silently. Their trick was to fly low and shut off the engines near their bombing target, taking the enemy by surprise.

WHY A HERO?

Nadya flew a very slow PO-2 biplane with two bombs, but no guns, radio, or parachute. She once flew 18 attacks in one night. Nadya was shot down three times, but continued flying until the end of the war.

> ## 66 Our planes were the slowest in the air force. They often came back riddled with bullets… 99

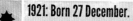
KEY DATES

⭐ 1921: Born 27 December.

🏆 1937: First solo flight, aged 16.

1941: Joined a regiment of all-female pilots and ground crew.

1945: Left army and married; became a flying instructor.

⚰️ 2013: Died 8 July.

Dressed to kill
Nadya carried a beetle lucky charm and liked to wear a blue silk scarf as a change from the flying jackets and man-size boots of a pilot.

JOHN BASILONE

In October 1942, in mud and rain on Guadalcanal Island, US Marines were battling for Henderson Field against the Japanese. Sergeant John Basilone knew the enemy would keep coming, wave after wave. He had to keep his machine gun firing. Basilone stood his ground, urging his men to hold on.

> **&& Never fear your enemy but always respect them. 99**

WHY A HERO?

At Guadalcanal, Basilone kept firing at the advancing Japanese. At one point he rushed forward to spray the enemy line with bullets from a Colt 45. Somehow the Americans held on as their sergeant refused to retreat. His stand was a key morale booster for the US Marines.

Headstrong hero
John Basilone returned to the US a hero, but after the medals and parades he insisted on returning to the war.

KEY DATES

1916: Born 4 November.

1940: Joined US Marine Corps.

1942: Fought at Guadalcanal.

1942: Awarded Medal of Honor.

1943: Returned home a hero but requested return to battle.

1945: Died 19 February, killed at Iwo Jima.

BHANBHAGTA GURUNG

Gurkha soldiers from Nepal in the Himalayas are famously brave. Bhanbhagta Gurung joined the British Army aged 18. By 1945, he was a war-hardened jungle soldier when, with astonishing courage, he single-handedly took on Japanese guns. He won the Victoria Cross medal for his heroism.

WHY A HERO?

Japanese sniper and machine-gun fire had Gurung and his companions pinned down. Gurung chose to rush forward alone – with rifle, bayonet, and grenades. He captured the enemy machine-gun bunker, and defended it with other soldiers as the Japanese tried to take it back.

> **66 His courageous clearing of five enemy positions... was in itself decisive... 99**
> **Victoria Cross citation**

Jungle warrior
Like all Nepalese Gurkha soldiers, Gurung was a skilful jungle fighter. He used guns and a traditional kukri knife.

KEY DATES

 1921: Born September.

 1943: Fought in Burma against the Japanese.

1945: Awarded Victoria Cross for battlefield heroism.

1946: Left army to care for his family.

 2008: Died 1 March.

CHARLES UPHAM

New Zealander Charles Upham was the only soldier to win the Victoria Cross medal twice in World War II. He won the first in Crete, May 1941, throwing hand grenades at German paratroopers, and carrying a wounded comrade to safety. The next day he himself was wounded, but carried on fighting.

> **He showed superb coolness, great skill and dash, and complete disregard of danger.**
> 1st Victoria Cross citation

WHY A HERO?

In 1942, at El Alamein, North Africa, Upham again attacked with grenades and was wounded. Keeping his nerve, he ordered enemy Italians to free his jeep, which was stuck in sand. Upham was taken prisoner and later imprisoned in Colditz Castle by the Germans.

KEY DATES

1908: Born 21 September.

1939: Served in New Zealand Expeditionary Force. During WWII, fought in Greece, Crete, Western Desert (North Africa).

1942–1945: Prisoner of war.

1946: Became a farmer in New Zealand.

1994: Died 22 November.

Hatless soldier
Upham's exploits showed outstanding courage. He fought without a helmet, claiming the army "tin hats" never fitted properly.

VASILY ZAITSEV

"Super-sniper" Vasily Zaitsev was hailed a Hero of the Soviet Union (USSR). Having learned to hunt as a boy, he was deadly with a rifle. Zaitsev's sharp-shooting killed at least 300 Germans.

WHY A HERO?

Zaitsev fought at the Battle of Stalingrad, 1942. He shot dead a German sniper in a window 800 m (half a mile) away, impressing his commander. He then became a sniper himself, hiding in rubble, ruins, and drainpipes to kill soldiers or enemy snipers.

66 We had to find him... and patiently await the moment for one shot. 99

KEY DATES

 1915: Born 23 March.

 1937: Joined the Red Army.

1941: Volunteered for the front line. Served on the Eastern Front (Russia and Ukraine).

1942: Battle of Stalingrad.

Post-1945: An engineer and factory manager.

 1991: Died 15 December.

Sniper trainer
Zaitsev was wounded in 1943. However, he returned to battle and passed on his sniper skills to other soldiers.

AUDIE MURPHY

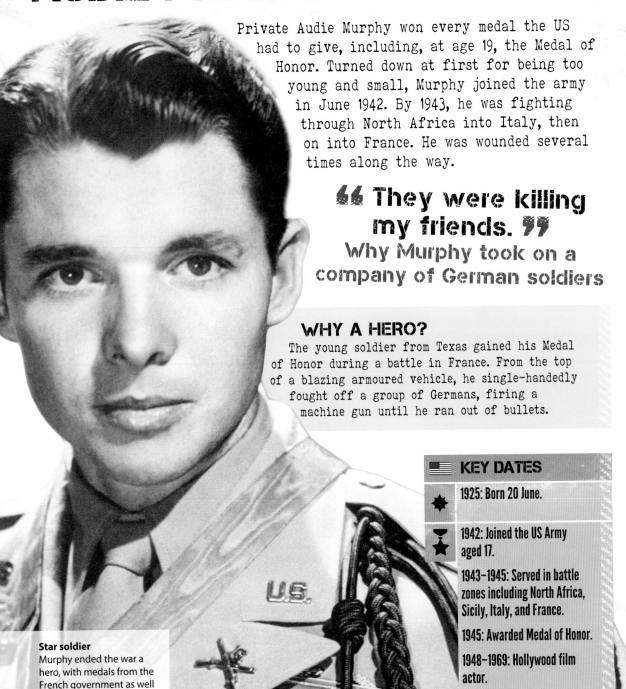

Private Audie Murphy won every medal the US had to give, including, at age 19, the Medal of Honor. Turned down at first for being too young and small, Murphy joined the army in June 1942. By 1943, he was fighting through North Africa into Italy, then on into France. He was wounded several times along the way.

66 They were killing my friends. 99
Why Murphy took on a company of German soldiers

WHY A HERO?

The young soldier from Texas gained his Medal of Honor during a battle in France. From the top of a blazing armoured vehicle, he single-handedly fought off a group of Germans, firing a machine gun until he ran out of bullets.

KEY DATES

1925: Born 20 June.

1942: Joined the US Army aged 17.

1943–1945: Served in battle zones including North Africa, Sicily, Italy, and France.

1945: Awarded Medal of Honor.

1948–1969: Hollywood film actor.

1971: Died 28 May.

Star soldier
Murphy ended the war a hero, with medals from the French government as well as his own. He later starred as an action hero in Hollywood films.

EDWARD KENNA

Private Edward "Ted" Kenna served in the Australian infantry, fighting the Japanese in New Guinea (May 1945). His platoon had orders to "deal with" a machine gun that was holding up the Allied advance. Due to Kenna's bravery, the Australians captured the gun post. He was awarded the Victoria Cross medal for his bravery.

WHY A HERO?

With the enemy almost upon them, Kenna stood up, firing his gun. As bullets flew past him and with no ammunition left, he called for a rifle. Kenna shot the machine gunner and his replacement.

❝ ... an outstanding example of the highest degree of bravery. ❞
Victoria Cross citation

KEY DATES

 1919: Born 6 July.

 1940: Joined Australian forces.

1944: Arrived in New Guinea.

1945: Awarded Victoria Cross.

1945: Wounded in action in June.

1946: Discharged from the forces.

 2009: Died 8 July.

Long road to recovery
Just three weeks after Kenna heroically helped to capture the gun post in New Guinea, he was badly wounded and spent a year recovering in hospital.

JAMES RUDDER

US Rangers had commando fighting skills, and James Rudder helped make them one of the war's most outstanding combat units. In June 1944, he led them onto Omaha Beach in Normandy, France, to open the way for the Allied landings of D-Day, and the liberation of Europe.

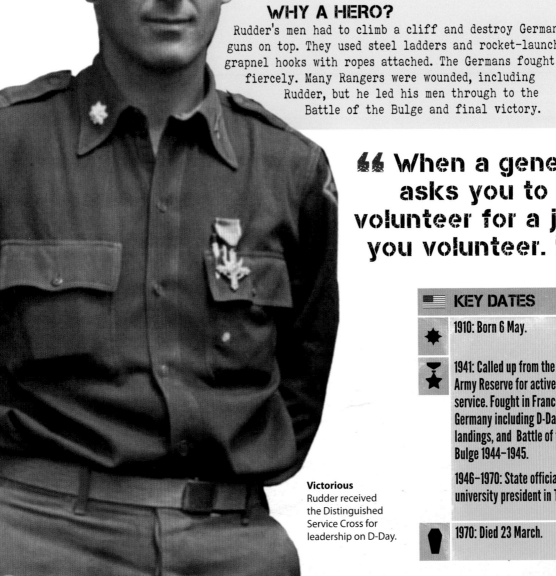

WHY A HERO?

Rudder's men had to climb a cliff and destroy German guns on top. They used steel ladders and rocket-launched grapnel hooks with ropes attached. The Germans fought fiercely. Many Rangers were wounded, including Rudder, but he led his men through to the Battle of the Bulge and final victory.

66 When a general asks you to volunteer for a job, you volunteer. 99

Victorious
Rudder received the Distinguished Service Cross for leadership on D-Day.

🇺🇸 KEY DATES

 1910: Born 6 May.

 1941: Called up from the US Army Reserve for active service. Fought in France and Germany including D-Day landings, and Battle of the Bulge 1944–1945.

1946–1970: State official and university president in Texas.

 1970: Died 23 March.

OTTO SKORZENY

Germany's most famous "secret soldier", Skorzeny led a hand-picked band of special-forces commandos. One mission, in 1943, was to rescue Italy's ousted leader, Mussolini. Skorzeny also fought at the Battle of the Bulge (1944-1945), where his men wore US uniforms and used metal sheets to disguise German tanks as US Sherman tanks.

WHY A HERO?

As Mussolini was held in a mountaintop hotel, Skorzeny and his 75 paratroopers used gliders for the rescue raid. Eight German gliders crash-landed. Skorzeny seized Mussolini and flew out with him, squashed together with a pilot, in a two-man light plane.

❝ You cannot waste time... You must decide on your target and go in. ❞

Well rewarded
Nazi leader Hitler personally chose Skorzeny to lead the Mussolini rescue mission. Skorzeny won the Iron Cross medal for his efforts.

KEY DATES

 1908: Born 12 June, in Austria.

 1931-1945: Served in the German Army.

1945-1948: Prisoner of war. Escaped and allegedly helped Nazis flee to South America.

 1975: Died 5 July.

JACK CHURCHILL

Many commandos like unusual weapons, but Jack Churchill was probably unique. In 1940, he shot arrows at German soldiers in France. He landed on the beaches of Italy in 1943, brandishing a sword. Sometimes, he even played the bagpipes while leading his commandos into battle!

WHY A HERO?

Jack Churchill led commando raids in Norway and joined the Allied landings in Italy where, with other British soldiers, he captured 42 of the enemy. In 1944, he was taken prisoner during a raid in Yugoslavia, but escaped.

" I will shoot that first German with an arrow... "

 KEY DATES

 1906: Born 16 September.

1926–1959: Served in the British Army.
World War II service included France 1939–1940 and commando raids 1941–1944.

1944: Captured and became a prisoner of war.

1959: Retired from army.

 1996: Died 8 March.

Sharp shooter
Although not related to the British prime minister, Jack Churchill was no less determined. He was the only WWII soldier known to have shot an enemy with a longbow.

JEAN MOULIN

Jean Moulin was a hero of the French Resistance, the secret "underground" army against the Nazis. He lost his civil service job in 1940 when German secret police arrested him as a Communist. Moulin escaped to England and joined the Free French movement under General Charles de Gaulle.

> **"He attained the limits of human suffering without betraying a single secret..."**

WHY A HERO?

Moulin returned to France and organized Maquis (French Resistance) groups into a secret army. With weapons from the Allies, they made sabotage raids on factories, railways, and German occupiers. But, in June 1943, a traitor betrayed him. Arrested and tortured to make him talk, Jean Moulin died in 1943.

KEY DATES

 1899: Born 20 June.

 1940: Dismissed from civil service by Vichy authorities for his anti-Nazi stand.

1941: Smuggled to Britain to join Free French.

1942: Parachuted into France to set up Resistance Council.

1943: Captured by Nazis.

 1943: Died 8 July, after being tortured.

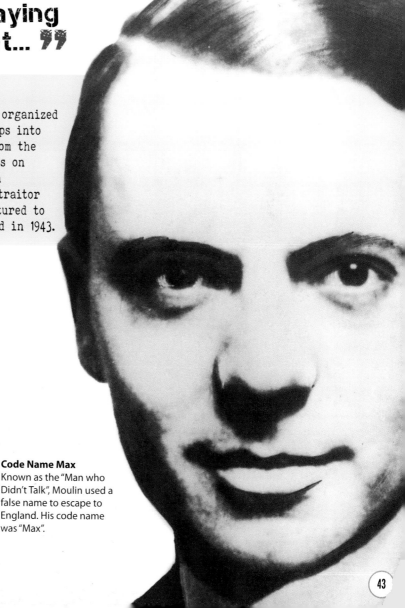

Code Name Max
Known as the "Man who Didn't Talk", Moulin used a false name to escape to England. His code name was "Max".

SPIES AND SECRET AGENTS

Every nation had its spies, code-makers, and code-breakers to uncover the military secrets that might bring victory. All worked in secrecy, listening to radio intercepts, reading stolen letters, and interrogating enemy prisoners. To aid Resistance groups fighting "underground war" in enemy-occupied countries, the Allies sent in brave men and women as secret agents. Theirs was perhaps the most nerve-racking and deadly war of all.

ODETTE SANSOM

Odette Sansom was a Frenchwoman living in England. In 1942, she was recruited by the British Special Operations Executive (SOE) as a secret agent, using her knowledge of France against the Nazis. She became one the most famous agents of WWII.

WHY A HERO?

In 1942, Odette was sent to France along with agent Peter Churchill. They fell in love, but Odette was captured. Tortured by the Gestapo, she kept silent, and was sent to a concentration camp. The Nazis' mistaken belief that she was married to a Churchill possibly saved her from being shot.

66 My comrades are not here to speak... I speak for them. 99

  KEY DATES

★ **1912:** Born 28 April.

1942: Volunteered as an SOE agent; received training.

1942–1943: SOE agent in France.

1943–1945: Prisoner of the Nazis, survived torture and imprisonment at Ravensbruck concentration camp.

1946: Awarded George Cross medal for bravery.

1995: Died 13 March.

Courageous agent
Odette won the George Cross medal for her courage. She stuck to her cover story despite being tortured.

JOAN PUJOL GARCIA

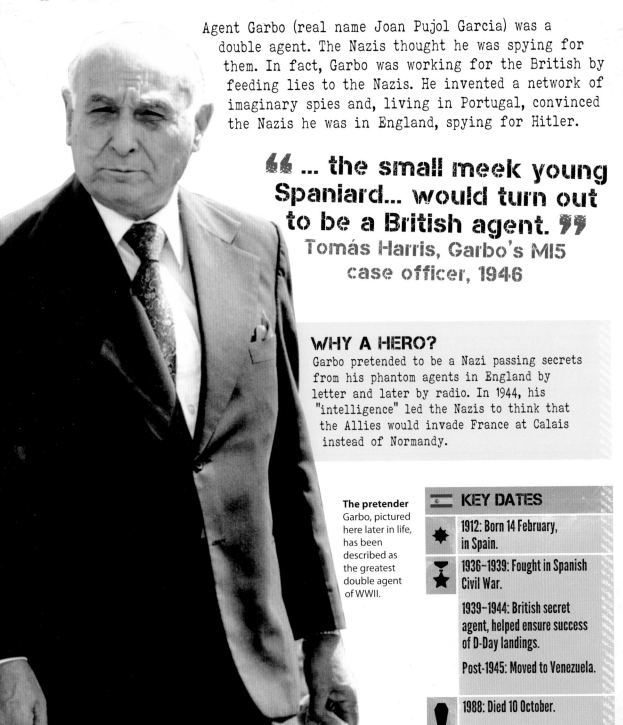

Agent Garbo (real name Joan Pujol Garcia) was a double agent. The Nazis thought he was spying for them. In fact, Garbo was working for the British by feeding lies to the Nazis. He invented a network of imaginary spies and, living in Portugal, convinced the Nazis he was in England, spying for Hitler.

> **66** ... the small meek young Spaniard... would turn out to be a British agent. **99**
> Tomás Harris, Garbo's MI5 case officer, 1946

WHY A HERO?

Garbo pretended to be a Nazi passing secrets from his phantom agents in England by letter and later by radio. In 1944, his "intelligence" led the Nazis to think that the Allies would invade France at Calais instead of Normandy.

The pretender
Garbo, pictured here later in life, has been described as the greatest double agent of WWII.

KEY DATES

1912: Born 14 February, in Spain.

1936–1939: Fought in Spanish Civil War.

1939–1944: British secret agent, helped ensure success of D-Day landings.

Post-1945: Moved to Venezuela.

1988: Died 10 October.

WITOLD PILECKI

Pilecki was one of many brave Poles facing both Nazi and Communist enemies. In 1939, German and Russian forces invaded Poland. Pilecki volunteered to join prisoners in Auschwitz concentration camp, and his secret messages told the outside world that the Nazis had begun mass killings of Jews.

WHY A HERO?

For more than two years, Pilecki's secret network sent out reports from Auschwitz. In 1943, he escaped to join Poles in the 1944 Warsaw Uprising. He was captured, but later joined a Free Polish Army troop. After the war, Pilecki returned to Poland, but was arrested by the Communists now running his country.

66 During the first three years, two million people were killed. 99
Pilecki's report on Auschwitz

Untold hero
Three years after the war ended, Pilecki was executed for being a spy. His story of courage was not fully told until Communist control of Poland collapsed in 1989.

KEY DATES

1901: Born 13 May.

1918: Served in Polish Army.

1939: Joined Polish Resistance.

1944: Captured by Nazis after Warsaw Rising.

1947: Imprisoned in Poland by Communists for "spying".

1948: Died 25 May, executed in Warsaw by Communists.

NANCY WAKE

While working undercover in France, Australian Nancy Wake knew no one could be trusted – even friends could turn out to be enemies. The German Gestapo offered a reward for her capture. If caught, Wake knew she would most likely be tortured, then shot.

> **" I don't see why we women should... wave our men... goodbye and then knit them balaclavas. "**

WHY A HERO?

Wake was living in France when the Nazis invaded (1940). She escaped to England, trained as an agent, then returned to help the French Resistance. She cycled around, carrying messages and helping to sabotage factories making Nazi war equipment.

Wanted
Nancy Wake became the Gestapo's most wanted person, but "The White Mouse" proved too hard to catch.

KEY DATES

 1912: Born 30 August.

 1940: Joined the French Resistance as a courier.

1944: Became a British SOE (Special Operations Executive) agent in Occupied France.

1949: Returned to Australia.

 2011: Died 7 August.

NOOR INAYAT KHAN

Known as "Agent Madeleine", Noor Inayat Khan was the first female radio operator sent secretly into Nazi-occupied France by the British. Khan was raised in Britain and France by her American father and Indian mother. In June 1943, she flew into France – and into danger.

WHY A HERO?

Khan was London's only link with her Resistance group after the Nazis seized other radio operators. She would not leave Paris, but was betrayed in October 1943. Although the Gestapo tortured her, Khan refused to talk.

66 Liberté (freedom). 99
Khan's final word before her execution

KEY DATES

1914: Born 1 January, in Moscow, Russia.

1940: Escaped from France to England.

1942: Joined SOE as an agent.

1943: Sent to France in June, captured in October.

1944: Died 13 September, shot in Dachau.

Brave to the end
After 10 months of torture and two failed escape attempts, Khan was sent to Dachau concentration camp. There, she was shot and killed in 1944.

HEROES OF THE HOLOCAUST

Hitler's Nazis persecuted Jews in every country they occupied. They sent special "death squads" to murder them, or rounded them up and shipped them by train to concentration camps and death camps, which had poison-gas chambers built for the mass killing of prisoners.

IRENA SENDLER

When the German army invaded Poland in 1939, Jews were prevented from leaving. From 1942, the occupying Nazis trapped thousands of Jews inside a ghetto in the capital city, Warsaw. Social worker Sendler went into the ghetto to report on conditions.

WHY REMEMBERED?

The Warsaw ghetto had 500,000 people crammed inside. Food was scarce, there was no medicine, and children were sick and dying. Sendler smuggled out more than 2,000 children to the care of non-Jews.

❝ You see a man drowning. You must try to save him... ❞

Save the children
Sendler smuggled Jewish children out of the ghetto in ambulances, sacks, and even a toolbox. She kept their names in a jar buried under a tree, hoping that one day they might find out who they really were.

RESCUE STORY

1910: Born 15 February.

Nationality: Polish

Rescue zone: Warsaw, Poland; member of Polish Resistance.

Post-war: Honoured in Israel as a hero.

2008: Died 12 May.

CHIUNE SUGIHARA

Japan was friendly towards Nazi Germany in 1940, but had not yet joined the war. Sugihara, a Japanese diplomat, saw Jews being persecuted in Lithuania. He was friends with a Jewish boy who had invited him home to meet his family. Sugihara decided to help Jews escape.

❝ There was no place else for them to go... ❞

WHY REMEMBERED?

Sugihara used his job at the Japanese embassy to issue "safe" travel passes to any Jew who wanted one. Hundreds of Jews left Lithuania by train, across Russia to Japan, then on to the US and even Palestine.

Friend in need
Sugihara gave a visa to his friend, Solly Ganor, but Solly did not manage to escape. Solly was sent to a Nazi concentration camp, but survived.

● RESCUE STORY

 1900: Born 1 January.

 Nationality: Japanese

Rescue zone: Lithuania 1939–1940.

1944: Arrested by Russians.

Post-war: Moved to Prague (Czechoslovakia); retired 1947.

 1986: Died 31 July.

GIORGIO PERLASCA

Rescuers of Holocaust victims risked their lives by hiding Jews or helping them escape the Nazis. Fear of prison or death did not stop Perlasca. An Italian diplomat, he helped Jews in Hungary flee Nazi persecution. He started when Italy changed sides in 1943.

WHY REMEMBERED?

The Nazis ordered Italians out of Hungary but Perlasca stayed on, working at the Spanish embassy. He issued travel passes to Jews and found them homes where they could hide. He also saved two boys from a death train by arguing with a German officer.

Undercover Italian
Perlasca stayed on at the embassy, pretending to be Spanish, even after the ambassador left. His brave actions saved more than 3,000 Jews from the gas chambers.

66 At first I didn't know what to do. 99

RESCUE STORY

1910: Born 31 January.

Nationality: Italian

Rescue zone: Hungary

Post-war: Went home to Italy; seldom talked of the war.

1992: Died 15 August.

OSKAR SCHINDLER

German businessman Oskar Schindler helped save the lives of many Jews during the Holocaust. He claimed to need them for work in his factories in Poland. Employees had to work hard, but Jews in Schindler's factories were safe.

WHY REMEMBERED?

Schindler used Jews from the Krakow ghetto as cheap labour, but then tried to protect his workers. When the Nazis tried to close the Polish factory, Schindler opened a new one in Czechoslovakia. He made a list of 1,200 Jewish workers needed, saving them from the death camps.

❝ I just couldn't stand by and see people destroyed. ❞

RESCUE STORY

 1908: Born 28 April.

 Nationality: German-Czech

Rescue zones: Poland and Czechoslovakia.

Post-war: Moved to Argentina; honoured by Israel 1963.

 1974: Died 9 October.

Life saver
Although a Nazi Party member, Schindler saved hundreds of Jews from the gas chambers at Auschwitz.

ANNE FRANK

Anne Frank was a teenager who kept a diary as she hid from the Nazis for two years. Her family were German Jews. To escape the Nazis they moved to the Netherlands. Then, in 1940, the Nazis invaded their new homeland. Danger grew, so, in 1942, the Franks and four friends went into hiding.

> **❝ I don't think of all the misery. But of the beauty that still remains. ❞**

WHY REMEMBERED?

Anne and her family hid in rooms behind Anne's father's office in Amsterdam. Miep Gies, who worked for Mr Frank, brought them food and supplies. Before being betrayed, Anne recorded a detailed diary of her life in hiding.

Diary rescue
Anne Frank, with her sister Margot, died in Bergen-Belsen camp in spring 1945. Miep rescued Anne's diary, and later gave it to Anne's father. Only he survived the Nazi death camps.

HER STORY

 1929: Born 12 June, Germany, but moved to the Netherlands.

 Nationality: German

In hiding: From July 1942. Captured in August 1944.

Post-war: Her diary first published in 1947.

 1945: Died early March in Bergen-Belsen camp.

CHAPTER TWO:
MILITARY PERSONNEL

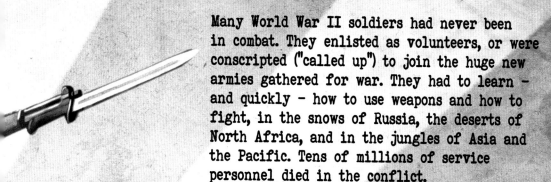

Many World War II soldiers had never been in combat. They enlisted as volunteers, or were conscripted ("called up") to join the huge new armies gathered for war. They had to learn — and quickly — how to use weapons and how to fight, in the snows of Russia, the deserts of North Africa, and in the jungles of Asia and the Pacific. Tens of millions of service personnel died in the conflict.

> **Never in the field of human conflict was so much owed by so many to so few.**
>
> British Prime Minister Winston Churchill speaking about the Battle of Britain

IN THIS CHAPTER:

This chapter presents personnel from the armed services of different nations. Ordinary men and women faced extraordinary situations in battles on land, at sea, and in the air. Most were trained with special skills for the job they had to do.

Soft bush hat

AUSTRALIAN INFANTRY RIFLEMAN

Australians fighting alongside British troops in 1939 found themselves far from home. By 1941, Australia itself was in danger. Japan had invaded the islands of the Pacific. In the jungle of New Guinea, Australian soldiers came face to face with the Japanese enemy.

TOUGH GOING

New Guinea's forested mountains saw fierce jungle warfare. Sweat-soaked soldiers slept rough and got drenched and bitten by insects as they hacked through tangled bush. An enemy could be behind the next tree – or in its branches, taking aim with a rifle.

Soldiers carried food and drinking water

WEAPONRY & KIT

Many Australians wore a bush hat, not a standard helmet.

A rifleman's chief weapon was his No. 1 SMLE .303 rifle. A bayonet attached to the rifle was a stabbing weapon for hand-to-hand combat.

A medical kit was always useful.

Rations and ammunition were carried in pouches.

Tough, hobnail leather ankle boots

Hard helmet

JAPANESE MACHINE GUNNER

Japanese soldiers were trained to obey without question. They also followed ancient codes of honour, such as "never surrender". To lay down their weapons was unthinkable. Allied soldiers found this hard to understand.

Rifle with bayonet attached

JUNGLE COMBAT

The Japanese became expert jungle fighters. Snipers lay in tree-tops, while machine-gunners hid weapons under leaves and branches. Japanese armies could march 30 km (18 miles) and live on less than 2 kg (1 lb) of food a day.

Woollen puttees protected from the cold and injury

● WEAPONRY & KIT

Japanese uniform included a helmet and leggings. Twigs and leaves made good camouflage.

The elderly Arisaka rifle had a very long bayonet for close fighting.

A Type 99 machine gun was light and fired 500 bullets a minute, an ideal ambush weapon.

SOVIET TANK DRIVER

Padded helmet

Warm underclothing

Overalls

Russia had more than 20,000 tanks and armoured vehicles in 1941, but lost many in early battles against German Panzer tanks. The T-34 tank was the Red (Soviet) Army's mainstay. Although tough, its engine soon wore out. Tank drivers would have to leap out to carry out quick repairs.

RED ARMY "TANKERS"

A T-34 tank had a four-man crew: commander, loader, gunner, and driver. Inside it was noisy, stuffy, and cramped. The driver peered through a slit. He tried to station the tank "hull-down" behind a mound. The body of the tank was hidden, but the turret gunner could see the enemy.

WEAPONRY & KIT

 Soviet tankers wore either a padded or a metal helmet, and overalls (with warm underclothing in cold conditions).

 Goggles were also worn for added protection both inside and outside the tank.

 Crews were ready to shoot if they had to bail out (jump clear of a burning tank). Many carried the Tokarev T-33 pistol.

GERMAN ANTI-TANK GUNNER

Panzerfaust

While infantrymen liked their own tanks – they provided shelter and firepower – enemy tanks sent most soldiers diving for cover. Some weapons could stop tanks, however. The German army used the panzerfaust ("tank fist" anti-tank missile launcher) from 1943, and an 88-mm gun that could "kill" any tank.

TANK-BLASTER

The anti-tank gunner hid in a building or behind a dirt bank. His panzerfaust was a basic metal tube that fired a "bomb" on the end of a wooden stick. It was light enough to carry, but could could blast a hole in armour 250 mm (10 in) thick.

Standard equipment included a water bottle and a blanket

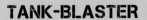 WEAPONRY & KIT

 Most German soldiers, including anti-tank gunners, wore the standard Wehrmacht helmet.

 German anti-tank gunners used the panzerfaust anti-tank weapon and the 88-mm gun, and rifle and grenades for close combat.

 The Nazi SS (Schutzstaffel) – Hitler's elite bodyguard – also used anti-tank weapons.

INDIAN GUNNER

Thousands of Indian Army soldiers fought with the Allies in Burma, North Africa, and through Sicily and Italy. Many belonged to infantry regiments and served as gunners in the artillery. The artillery big guns were important in WWII battles. Their job was to destroy enemy defences and so open the way for infantry and tanks to move forward.

Gunners had no ear protectors to muffle gunfire

Shorts were worn in hotter climates

BIG GUNS AND SMALL

The artillery had to move across country as battle raged, pulling their heavy guns into position with trucks, tractors, horses, or (in the jungle) elephants. Before a big attack, artillery fired high-explosive shells in massive barrages. At close range, gunners fired smaller mortars, lobbing shells into the air and onto the enemy.

WEAPONRY & KIT

Indian soldiers following the Sikh religion wore a traditional turban, or "dastaar", not a helmet.

The big guns were often fired in batteries (groups). Gunners worked together to load, aim, and fire the shells, then reload.

The big guns fired shells weighing 11.5 kg (25 lb), which crashed down on the enemy.

ITALIAN INFANTRYMAN

The Italian Army's infantry included Bersaglieri, the famous marksmen who wore feathered hats and marched at a trot. In the desert they wore loose cotton clothing and sun helmets. Many Italian soldiers in North Africa were new recruits, ill-prepared for desert warfare.

Standard uniform, made of wool

Many Italian soldiers still had old 6-shot rifles

DESERT RIDERS

Mobility was the key to desert battles. Soldiers in trucks moved faster than those on foot, but for extra speed, both sides used motorcycle messengers. Bike riders carried vital battlefield orders to the firing line.

WEAPONRY & KIT

Bersaglieri marksmen stuck cockerel feathers into their metal helmets.

Italian infantry used the Solothurn anti-tank rifle and the handy Beretta 34 pistol. Many soldiers still had old 6-shot rifles.

Infantry in North Africa were "mechanized", riding on tanks, cars, and motorbikes.

BRITISH NAVY DESTROYER CAPTAIN

Destroyers were small, fast warships. They hunted submarines, escorted convoys of cargo ships, and guarded bigger vessels. The captain of a destroyer had to use his wits in fast-changing situations to keep his ship and men safe, and to sink the enemy.

Ceremonial sword

BATTLE STATIONS

From the ship's bridge, the captain spoke to the engine room, the gunners, and crew in charge of torpedoes and depth charges. The ship had three "watch-keepers" at all times. If an enemy ship was spotted, the captain ordered "battle stations" to send the crew into action.

White ceremonial dress was worn for ceremonial occasions. Regular uniform was navy blue.

⚓ WEAPONRY & KIT

 Both captain and crew wore thick sweaters, duffel coats, warm socks, and boots for freezing, stormy weather.

 Naval guns, anti-aircraft guns, torpedoes, and depth charges were a destroyer captain's weapons.

 The captain viewed the sea and sky through binoculars.

U-BOAT COMMANDER ATLANTIC

The German Navy tried to cut off Allied supplies by attacking cargo ships using submarines (U-boats). Armed with guns and torpedoes, every U-boat commander played "cat and mouse" with enemy ships as they hunted them. U-boat "ace" Otto Kretschmer sank 47 Allied ships in 18 months.

Submarine sailors wore light clothes in the hot, cramped vessel

WOLF PACKS

U-boat commanders spent weeks on patrol at sea. In groups known as "wolf packs", they hunted for enemy convoys or lone ships. If warships were with the convoy, the commander could surface his submarine, and sink the target with gunfire.

WEAPONRY & KIT

Captains viewed targets through a periscope.

The U-boat had at least 22 torpedoes, fired from tubes at the bow (front) or stern (back).

Aboard his U-boat, a commander wore a peaked cap with a white cover.

Flying goggles

USAAF B-17 GUNNER

American B-17 bombers attacked in flights of around 54 planes. Each B-17 had 10 crew and 13 machine guns. The gunner sat behind a Browning gun, firing 14 bullets a second to hit a fighter up to 550 m (0.3 miles) away. Many who tried failed the B-17 fitness test, unable to stand the high altitude at which the plane flew.

Emergency life jacket in case of sea landing

DAYLIGHT RAIDS

A gunner's life was tough and dangerous. It was cramped and freezing cold. Flying in daylight, the bombers were easy to see, but very high. Wind whipped through the bomber - and so did enemy bullets.

WEAPONRY & KIT

B-17 gunners wore heated suits, boots, gloves, and a helmet with oxygen mask and intercom.

A skilled gunner fired short, sharp bursts. He knew he could keep firing for just a minute before running out of bullets.

Each B-17 carried 9,000 rounds of ammunition for its Browning machine guns.

Leather jacket for warmth at high altitude

LUFTWAFFE FIGHTER PILOT

Pilots of the Luftwaffe, the German Air Force, had many victories in the first part of the war. Flying in fighters such as the Me-109, the top-scoring fighter-pilot "ace" was a national hero - such as Adolf Galland. With 70 victories by June 1941, he became a general aged just 30.

ACE FIGHTER

Pilots in the Focke-Wulf Fw-190 were a match for anyone. A new fighter in 1941, this plane was faster than the British Spitfire. Roaring into combat at top speeds of more than 600 kph (372 mph), its pilots challenged Allied bombers over Germany. Yet even ace German pilots faced overwhelming odds as Allied airpower grew.

Deep pockets for maps and escape kit

WEAPONRY & KIT

Fighter pilots wore leather combat jackets. Like many Allied pilots, they wore soft scarves around their necks.

Flying trousers had big thigh pockets for notebooks, maps, orders, and escape kits.

Pilots communicated by radio. Ground control told the pilot where to attack enemy bombers.

Leather boots

RAF BOMBER PILOT

Royal Air Force pilots made night-time raids over Germany from 1940. This meant flying for up to 1,600 km (1,000 miles), a trip lasting many hours. A pilot and his crew had to find the target, dodge enemy guns and fighters, drop the bombs, then head for home.

READY TO RAID

A pilot was told the night's target at noon. He was then in charge of the plane and crew. His navigator studied the route. The engineer and radio operator tested their kit, and the air gunners checked guns. Bombs were loaded as the crew relaxed, waiting for darkness.

Flying helmet with a built-in radio

"Mae West" life jacket in case crew were shot down over water

🇬🇧 WEAPONRY & KIT

Airmen took medical packs and escape kits to use if shot down.

Some bombers had chemical bucket-toilets, but no one liked them. Many fliers used bottles instead.

As well as "battledress" RAF uniform, life jackets, and flying helmets, crew wore two pairs of socks (wool and silk), and wool-lined flying boots.

GERMAN ENGINEER

Army engineers helped units to move forwards. They built roads, airstrips, and bridges. They also set up radio and telephone communications. As the army's explosives experts, German engineers were good at pulling down buildings. They could blow up a bridge, lay a smoke screen to hide soldiers from the enemy, and set booby traps. They were also fighting soldiers.

FIGHTING GEAR

Engineers trained and fought as infantry, with rifles, pistols, and other weapons. They were specialists with all kinds of explosives, including land mines buried beneath the ground. German army "Pioneer" engineers were trained to use flame-throwers in combat.

German helmet

Smoke grenade

WEAPONRY & KIT

Engineers wore a regulation steel helmet or a field cap.

Their standard weapon was a German Army Mauser 98 rifle or carbine.

They were equipped with smoke grenades. These created clouds of chemical smoke to confuse the enemy and hide what was going on.

BRITISH COMMANDO

Commandos were British soldiers trained for surprise raids on the enemy. Soldiers volunteered for commando training, learning to climb cliffs, cross rivers, land on beaches from boats, and hide out in enemy territory. A commando moved silently, was hard to spot (wearing camouflage and blackened face at night), and could kill with his bare hands. Churchill loved commandos. Hitler hated them so much he ordered any captured commando to be shot.

HIT AND RUN

Army kit was adapted for "hit and run" raids. Commandos wore green berets, packed their kit in rucksacks, and carried "Roman swords" - long, vicious knives. Commando raiders made a bold attack on the port of Nazaire, France, in 1942. In 1944, they were some of the first Allied troops ashore in Normandy on D-Day.

WEAPONRY & KIT

 A commando had to be fit to carry more than 45 kg (100 lb) of kit, including weapons.

 Weapons included the quick-firing Thompson (Tommy gun) and the De Lisle carbine fitted with a silencer.

 A commando Fairbairn-Sykes fighting knife was worn on the leg.

Thick wool trousers

Gaiters worn around the ankles to keep out mud

FRENCH RESISTANCE FIGHTER

France was taken over by the Nazis in 1940. While occupied, it was a divided nation. The Germans ruled in the north. The south had a French government at Vichy, collaborating with the Nazis. Some French men and women left for England to join the Free French forces. Others joined the "underground" army called the Maquis.

Fighters had old guns and newer weapons supplied by Allies

French Resistance armband

FIGHTING BACK

Maquis resistance fighters used whatever weapons they had to shoot German troop trucks, sabotage factory machines, and blow up railways and telephone lines. They sent radio messages to the Allies, who airdropped weapons to help in the fight.

▮▮ WEAPONRY & KIT

 Maquis fighters had old guns from WWI, but also modern weapons sent from Britain.

 A small pistol such as the MAS 1935A was easy to hide in a pocket or bag.

 Explosive "sock-bombs" (a sock filled with explosive and greased with oil on the outside) could be stuck on enemy vehicles.

US MARINE

The motto of the US Marine Corps is "Always Faithful". Marines were trained for amphibious assaults - attack from the sea. They saw themselves as special. They had their own air force, and weapons that often differed slightly from those of the US Army. Marines trained hard. This was vital in helping them to win some of the Pacific war's bloodiest battles.

Marines carried similar kit to the US Army

Combat trousers

Sturdy leather boots

ON LAND AND SEA

Marines took landing craft ashore from Navy ships. Splashing onto the beach, they dug shallow holes in which to shelter from enemy gunfire. They had to fight their way off the beach, using guns, grenades, and flamethrowers. Marines kept advancing until the enemy had been killed or surrendered.

WEAPONRY & KIT

Like every soldier, Marines wore a dog tag (identity disc) on a cord around the neck. The disc bore their name, rank, and military service number.

Marines had the M1 Garand semi-automatic rifle, able to fire eight shots before it needed reloading.

Their ammunition belt had 10 pouches, with one clip (eight rifle bullets) in each pouch.

JAPANESE TEISHIN PARATROOPER

The Japanese Army and Navy each had its own paratroopers (military parachutists). Army paras were named Teishin, meaning "dash forward". The Teishin were trained to do enemy raids, or to land behind enemy lines and cut off or surround them. Japanese paras captured Palembang airfield in Indonesia from the Allies in 1942, and also fought in Burma.

Ammo and explosives in pouches

DASHING RAIDERS

Teishin usually dropped with only light weapons such as grenades and pistols. However, special engineer units carried flamethrowers and demolition charges (explosives). Kit later included light tanks and field guns, landed by glider.

In the early part of the war, Teishin uniform was similar to that of German Luftwaffe paratroopers

WEAPONRY & KIT

Paratroopers wore a parachute helmet, often German style – the Japanese studied German and Allied parachute tactics.

Teishin had two parachutes. They often ditched the reserve once the main parachute opened.

A favourite para weapon was a light sub-machine gun called the Type 100. It fired 30 rounds before reloading.

GURKHA CHINDIT

Gurkha soldiers from Nepal were among Allied "Chindits" fighting in the jungles of Burma against the Japanese. Formed by British General Orde Wingate, the Chindits went into battle in 1942 as guerrillas behind enemy lines. Japanese troops outnumbered the Chindits, but rarely saw them until the hidden guerrillas began firing, or set off explosives.

Floppy bush hat

Rifle or Sten gun

JUNGLE LIONS

Named after a Burmese mythical beast, the Chindits learned to be expert jungle fighters. Tramping across mountains and rivers, they carried their own kit, and kept in contact by field radio. The fighters came out of the forest exhausted, dirty, and often sick or wounded.

WEAPONRY & KIT

Many Chindits wore floppy bush hats. Clothing got torn, wet, and dirty in the jungle.

Gurkha Chindits attacked silently with a kukri, or knife, rather than a gun.

The Sten, a fast-firing light machine gun, was good for an ambush attack.

US MARAUDER

Merrill's Marauders (now known as Unit Galahad) were 3,000 US soldiers who, in 1943, volunteered for a dangerous mission. Specially trained in marksmanship and jungle survival skills, they were led by General Frank Merrill into Burma to help re-open the Burma Road, the vital Allied supply route to China.

Hard hat

NO PRISONERS

The Marauders began a 1,600-km (1,000-mile) trek on foot through the jungle. They fought five big battles, in one capturing Myitkina airfield from the Japanese. No other US soldiers marched so far or fought so much in so short a time. They left no wounded behind, carrying every injured man out on a stretcher.

Marauders weapons

🇺🇸 WEAPONRY & KIT

A Marauder carried kit on his back or on a pack mule.

Worn around the waist, the bandolier was used to carry grenades and other ammunition.

Medical kits had dressings, plaster tape, safety pins, scissors, iodine swabs, and forceps.

US PARATROOPER

US Army paratroopers of the famed 82nd and 101st Airborne divisions battled from Normandy to the Rhine in 1944–1945. Most jumped from C-47 planes, each with 28 men. Weighed down by kit, paras could easily crash-land, drown in a river or canal, or smash into trees. They might also be shot while drifting to the ground.

Army helmet (some had a net for camouflage)

GO! GO! GO!

Paratroopers could barely walk to their plane under the weight of their kit. On board, men sat facing one another, faces smeared with burnt cork camouflage. Once over the drop zone, they hooked "static lines" to an overhead cable. At the green light signal, one by one they span out of the aircraft doors. The static line yanked open the parachute.

First aid pack and emergency rations

WEAPONRY & KIT

Airborne troops fired shoulder-held bazookas to hit enemy tanks and bunkers.

Although they carried a compass, many paratroopers still got lost.

Tin "cricket" clicker to communicate in the dark (two clicks = friend).

Jumpsuit trousers with pockets and ties for kit

GERMAN PANZERGRENADIER

Panzer means "tank" or "armour", and a Panzergrenadier was a motorized infantry fighter. As part of a Blitzkrieg attack force, he rode into battle on a half-tracked armoured troop carrier or tank. Panzergrenadiers fought with a speed and punch that won them many victories alongside German Army tanks over western Europe and Russia.

M42 metal helmet, often with camouflage net

Wool toque or scarf around neck (useful as face mask)

Camouflage smock worn over army shirt

FAST AND FURIOUS

These soldiers fought with grenades, but many other weapons too, including FG 42 rifles and MP 38 sub-machine guns. The tough troops won a name for fierce fighting both in fast, furious attacks and, from 1944 to 1945, in last-ditch defence of Germany as Allied armies closed in.

WEAPONRY & KIT

German stick grenade, called a "potato masher" by the British.

Panzergrenadiers wore camouflage smocks, "spring" patterned on one side and "autumn" on the other, with white smocks for winter snow.

The MK43 carbine fired 30 rounds at a time. The soldier could add a curved barrel to shoot around corners.

JAPANESE NAVY PILOT

Flying goggles

Japan's powerful aircraft carrier fleet included big ships with space for more than 80 planes. Their Navy pilots flew dive bombers, torpedo bombers, and fighters. They trained for nine months and, when first pitched against US pilots in 1941, the Japanese had far more combat experience.

Japanese Rising Sun armband

STRIKE FORCE

Only the best were allowed to join the Japanese Navy. If trainee pilots made a mistake, instructors hit them with a stick. Pilots soon learned to obey orders. Showing off was bad; team spirit was good. As the Japanese Navy suffered defeats, it lost its best pilots. It threw in novice pilots and "kamikaze" fliers, who were ready to die.

● WEAPONRY & KIT

Pilots wore scarves of parachute silk. Kamikaze pilots on suicide missions waved these white scarves in farewell as they left.

The main Japanese dive bomber was the Aichi D3A (known as "Val" to the Allies). It sunk more Allied ships than any other Axis plane.

Every pilot had a notebook to record each mission. Pilots wrote goodbye letters to their families, knowing they might not return.

US AIRCRAFT CARRIER OFFICER

Deck personnel wore colour-coded headgear to indicate diffferent jobs

An aircraft carrier's planes depended on deck teams. Before launch, the carrier turned into the wind. Using an elevator, the deckmen moved the planes up from the hangar below deck. To position the planes ready for take-off, they waved paddles to signal to the pilots over the deafening roar of engines.

CLEAR THE DECKS!

When the planes returned, deckmen and controllers guided each pilot in to land. "Arrester wires" across the deck stopped planes from skidding over the side. Deck crews fought fires when damaged planes crash-landed. They shoved wrecks into the sea to clear the deck for the next landing.

Loose, light trousers

WEAPONRY & KIT

Sailors in the warm Pacific kept cool in light clothing, with naval caps.

For fire-fighting, deck crew had fire hoses and extinguishers.

Paddles were used to signal to pilots in order to position the planes for take-off and guide them in to land.

CHAPTER THREE:
KEY EVENTS & BATTLES

Battles in World War II were fought at sea, in the air, and on land. Some involved many thousands of people in combat, others were small-scale encounters played out in remote battle zones. Key events shaped the war, from the fall of France and the Battle of Britain in 1940 to the destruction of Nazi Germany and the atomic bombs that brought Japan's surrender in 1945.

**"Let no heart be faint.
Let every arm be steeled."**

Admiral Chester Nimitz
before the Battle of Leyte, 1944

IN THIS CHAPTER:

THE WAR IN EUROPE

On 1 September 1939 at 4.45am, Hitler ordered a German attack on Poland. On 3 September, Britain and France – Poland's allies – declared war on Germany. Australia, New Zealand, and Canada prepared for war, to help Britain. Many people hoped the war in Europe would be short, but what began in Poland in 1939 spread to the USSR and Asia, and by 1941 to the Pacific.

BLITZKRIEG

Blitzkrieg ("lightning war") was a new style of hard-hitting, fast-moving warfare first used by the Nazis in Poland in 1939. The shock tactics, involving bombing raids from the air while tanks smashed their way forward on the ground, forced the Poles to surrender after just 36 days of fighting.

FAST FACTS

 Radio communication was key to the success of Blitzkrieg, enabling aircraft to respond quickly to orders.

 In 1940, France had 3,000 tanks, against Germany's 2,500.

 The Allies had 13,000 big guns, almost twice as many as the Germans.

Tanks on the ground were supported by divebombers, such as the Junkers Ju 87, in the air

German troops rode on armoured vehicles

Advance into Belgium
Barbed wire was no obstacle as German tanks advanced through Belgium in 1940. The country surrendered on 28 May.

German StuGIII assault gun, built on a tank body

THE CONQUEST OF EUROPE

In April 1940, German armies poured into Denmark and Norway. In May, they rapidly overran Belgium, the Netherlands, and Luxembourg. Continuing west, they broke through French defences. On 14 June, Germans occupied Paris.

DUNKIRK RESCUE

The rapid advance of German armies in 1940 left thousands of Allied soldiers trapped at the French port of Dunkirk. Between 26 May and 4 June, 340,000 British, French, and Belgian troops were evacuated by a fleet of ships before the port fell to the Germans.

FAST FACTS

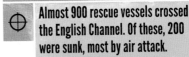
Almost 900 rescue vessels crossed the English Channel. Of these, 200 were sunk, most by air attack.

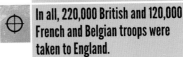
In all, 220,000 British and 120,000 French and Belgian troops were taken to England.

The smallest of the volunteer "Little Ships" was just 4.4 m (14 ft) long.

> **"** ...the Battle of France is over. The Battle of Britain is about to begin.**"**
> Winston Churchill, 18 June 1940

Many soldiers had to wade into the sea, up to their necks, again and again, before getting into a boat

Big ships waited offshore to pick up men ferried out by smaller boats

OPERATION DYNAMO

The codename for the evacuation of Dunkirk was Operation Dynamo. At first it was feared that only some of the troops could be evacuated in time, but the Royal Navy fleet was joined by hundreds of British volunteers in small fishing boats, sailing yachts, and steamers, who helped ferry men to safety.

Waiting for rescue
Lines of waiting soldiers stretched along the beaches. As the men huddled in the sand, bombs dropped by the Luftwaffe exploded all around them, and on the rescue boats.

BATTLE OF BRITAIN

In June 1940, Britain stood alone against the Nazis, but the country's new leader, Winston Churchill, ruled out peace-dealing with Germany. To try to force Britain out of the war, Hitler ordered air attacks on RAF airfields and the Battle of Britain began.

Hurricane force
The Hawker Hurricane was the chief fighter plane of the Battle of Britain. When German bombers were spotted, squadrons would take to the skies.

THE FEW
The RAF had fewer than 500 airworthy fighters against 1,500 German planes. But RAF Hurricanes and Spitfires proved a match for the German aircraft. Radar stations along the British coast, warning of incoming bombers, were also crucial.

OPERATION BARBAROSSA

"Barbarossa" was Hitler's code name for the invasion of the USSR in June 1941. He dreamed of defeating Communism and controlling all of Europe. At first the German attack was successful, but a combination of severe winter weather and determined Soviet counter-attacks brought the German advance to a halt.

German gunner takes aim

HEAVY CASUALTIES

Fighting in the USSR was savage. In the first six months alone, the Germans lost 750,000 men, either killed or wounded. Soviet losses were about 3.5 million dead and 3.5 million taken prisoner.

Gunning for victory
German field gunners captured the city of Kharkov, Ukraine, in 1941. However, the invading armies failed to take Leningrad (St Petersburg) or Moscow, the two main Soviet cities.

FAST FACTS

⊕ Germany sent an army of 4 million soldiers to invade the USSR.

⊕ The German forces of Operation Barbarossa had 3,000 tanks, 2,500 aircraft, and 7,000 artillery guns.

⊕ In 1942, 24,000 tanks and armoured vehicles were made in the USSR and 9,300 in Germany.

STALINGRAD

Throughout 1942 the Germans advanced into the USSR until they reached the city of Stalingrad. Here, they became locked in a desperate battle with Soviet troops. The fighting lasted five months, until the Germans surrendered. It was a turning point in the war. No longer was the German army invincible.

FAST FACTS

 More than 90,000 Germans were captured at Stalingrad. Most died in Soviet prison camps.

 About 800,000 Germans and Axis soldiers (mostly Romanian, Hungarian, and Italian) were killed.

 The Russian official losses were more than 1 million dead.

Street fighting
Soviet troops fought street by street to stop the Germans taking control of Stalingrad. There were heavy losses on both sides and the city was reduced to rubble.

TRAPPED

German troops advanced into Stalingrad, but became surrounded by Soviet forces. They tried to hold out, surviving on limited air drops of supplies. Against Hitler's orders, but with his men starving and no hope of rescue, the German commander, Field Marshal Paulus, surrendered.

BATTLE OF KURSK

In July 1943, German forces attacked Kursk, where Soviet troops were gathered at a key point on the eastern front line. It was the biggest tank battle in history. For every German tank destroyed, the Soviets lost five, but the tanks kept coming, eventually forcing the Germans into retreat. The battle was a turning point in the war on the Eastern Front.

OUTNUMBERED

German Panthers had thick armour and a gun that could penetrate all Allied tanks. Soviet shells bounced off them. But the Germans did not have enough "super-tanks" to match the huge numbers of Soviet T-34s.

German Panther

Soviet T-34

Soldiers faced attacks from the air as well as from the ground

On the move
Tanks advanced across the plains at Kursk where they engaged in huge battles. The air became thick with dust and smoke, and the fields were left littered with the wrecks of burnt-out vehicles.

FAST FACTS

⊕ The forces of the two sides together at Kursk totalled more than 2 million men, 6,000 tanks, and 5,000 aircraft.

⊕ In places along the likely route of the German advance, the Soviets placed 100 guns every kilometre (0.6 mile).

⊕ The Russians fired so many Katyusha rockets at Kursk that they set fire to the vast wheat fields of the steppes.

THE WARSAW GHETTO UPRISING

From 1939, the Nazis began rounding up Jews in occupied countries and forced them into prison camps or closed-off areas called ghettos. In 1942, the Nazis started to empty the ghettos, deporting the Jews to so-called "work camps". But when troops tried to empty the Warsaw ghetto in 1943, the defiant Jews rose up, refusing to surrender. The Germans returned in force to destroy the ghetto.

Jewish men, women, and children of Warsaw are rounded up by German soldiers, May 1943

POLISH UPRISING

In July 1944, Poles in Warsaw thought the arrival of the Soviet Army, and their freedom, was imminent. When the Nazis ordered 100,000 Poles to work on city defences, they refused and took to the streets. This second Warsaw Uprising also ended in terror. Nazi troops stormed the city, murdering civilians and burning buildings.

❝ There isn't a single wall intact... the beast's anger was terrible. ❞
Vasily Grossman, journalist

FAST FACTS

⊕ The walls of the Warsaw ghetto were more than 3 m (10 ft) high and 18 km (11 miles) long.

⊕ About 350,000 Jews lived in Warsaw, about 30 per cent of the population. When they were moved into the ghetto, it was 20 times more densely populated than the rest of the city.

⊕ In the Warsaw ghetto uprising, the Jews held out for three weeks.

Deportation
When the Jews were rounded up, they were told they were going to be resettled in the East. In fact, they were being deported to death camps, in which most of them did not survive.

D-DAY

On 6 June 1944, known as D-Day, a vast fleet of ships crossed from England to land an invasion force in Normandy, France. With the help of paratroopers, who had gone ahead to seize key positions, the Allies battled ashore.

FAST FACTS

⊕ The invasion force included 672 ships and 4,000 landing craft, under the protection of 13,000 aircraft.

⊕ Almost 156,000 Allied troops landed in France: 73,000 Americans, 62,000 British, and 21,000 Canadians.

⊕ Known as Operation Overlord, the D-Day invasion marked the beginning of the liberation of Western Europe.

Soldiers carried heavy packs and weapons

NORMANDY BEACHES

The landings took place on five beaches, codenamed Utah, Omaha, Gold, Juno, and Sword. Only at Omaha Beach (right) did things go wrong. There, US soldiers were pinned down on the narrow shore. German gunfire killed 2,000 on Omaha, more than on the other four D-Day beaches put together.

Onto the beach
The beaches where the Allied troops landed were defended by German forces. Landing craft went as close as they could; then, the ramp at the front was lowered and the soldiers waded ashore, often under enemy fire.

> **"Your task will not be an easy one... but we will accept nothing less than full victory."**
> US General Eisenhower

JULY BOMB PLOT

By 1944, a group of German officers believed defeat was inevitable. The Nazi leadership showed no intention of surrendering, so they decided to assassinate Hitler. Their plan was to make peace with the Allies. Colonel von Stauffenberg planted a bomb in Hitler's HQ, but the German leader survived.

> **❝ What was that? I am alive, I am alive! ❞**
> **Adolf Hitler**

Lucky escape
Hitler showed the wrecked meeting room to the Italian dictator Mussolini. Hitler said his escape was to save him for final victory.

Hitler inspects the bomb damage

A MIRACULOUS ESCAPE

Stauffenberg, a war hero with one eye and hand, took the bomb in a briefcase to a meeting with Hitler. He slipped it under a table, then drove away. Four people were killed in the explosion, but Hitler escaped unscathed. The leading conspirators, including Stauffenberg, were executed.

FAST FACTS

⊕ German generals first tried to blow up Hitler in a plane in March 1943.

⊕ The plotters may have asked Rommel to help. Afterwards, the Nazis forced him to kill himself.

⊕ The plotters' only chance of success was for Hitler to die, and then they could move quickly to take over.

PARIS LIBERATED

After D-Day, on 6 June 1944, Allied armies advanced into France. Progress was slow at first. The Germans fought hard for key cities such as Cherbourg and Caen, but in July the Allies broke through. Their drive towards Paris, the French capital, was led by US General George Patton.

FAST FACTS

- On 19 August 1944, the French flag flew again in Paris as Resistance fighters tore down German swastikas.

- On 25 August 1944, Free French and US soldiers marched into the city.

- More than one million people flocked to the centre of Paris on 26 August to celebrate their liberation.

ADVANCE INTO EUROPE

Through August 1944, Allied forces moved across France and Belgium, while a separate Allied landing was made in southern France. Brussels, the Belgian capital, was liberated on 3 September 1944. But then German resistance stiffened and the Allies faced a long, hard fight through the following winter.

Free at last!
Parisians celebrated the end of four years of occupation, and welcomed General de Gaulle, leader of the Free French.

ARNHEM

In September 1944, the Allies set their sights on Germany. British Field Marshal Montgomery planned a bold attack to seize key river bridges in the German-occupied Netherlands. This would allow Allied tanks to advance into Germany. However, the last bridge at Arnhem was not taken and the operation failed.

FAST FACTS

- On 17 September, 20,000 Allied airborne troops landed behind the Germans to cross the Rhine.

- The British forces' radios broke down during the attack, leaving them unable to communicate with each other or with HQ.

- More than 1,000 airborne soldiers were killed in the fighting, and 6,000 were taken prisoner.

OPERATION MARKET GARDEN

Montgomery's plan, known as Operation Market Garden, involved dropping troops by parachute to hold the vital river crossings until the tanks arrived. But at Arnhem, German forces were stronger than expected. Without ground support, the airborne troops suffered heavy casualties and were forced to surrender.

On the ground
British, US, and Polish paratroopers lacked heavy guns and tanks to fight off the Germans.

US paratroopers under heavy fire from Germans during Operation Market Garden

BATTLE OF THE BULGE

In December 1944, Hitler ordered one last counter-attack. In an offensive that became known as the Battle of the Bulge, he sent tanks into the Ardennes in Belgium, to break through the Allied front line. The German attack succeeded at first, but was resisted by well-organized and brave fighting.

FAST FACTS

 As US troops defended the town of Bastogne in Belgium, the Germans called upon them to surrender. Their commander replied, "Nuts".

 Around 19,000 US soldiers died in the Battle of the Bulge – the costliest battle of the war for the Americans.

 The offensive was over by 25 January 1945. The German losses were severe, with more than 100,000 men killed or wounded.

Into Belgium
The early success of the German assault led them to believe that they would deal the Allies a crippling blow.

German soldiers armed with rifles and stick grenades

SURPRISE IN THE SNOW

The offensive began on 16 December. The Germans disguised their tanks as American, and Germans wearing captured US uniforms sneaked past the Allied line. With bad weather grounding Allied planes, the Germans advanced 80 km (50 miles). But when the skies cleared, the Allies were able to destroy German tanks and trucks.

STRATEGIC BOMBING

Before the war, some people said no city could survive sustained bombing raids. Citizens would panic, stop working, or be killed – but the German Blitz on Britain (1940–1941) showed that life carried on. However, it was Allied bombers' attacks on German factory cities, especially in the Ruhr region, that would help win the war.

FAST FACTS

 Britain's Lancaster, Halifax, and Stirling bombers had fewer guns and less armour than US bombers.

 The US B-17 Flying Fortress dropped more than 640,000 tonnes of bombs, more than any other US aircraft.

Bombers targeted factories, power stations, and fuel dumps, but also had a disastrous effect on German cities.

CITY BUSTING

It was hard to hit targets from a high-flying bomber, so pilots tried "area-bombing" cities. The British attacked by night, and the US by day. Large-scale raids began in 1942, with a 900-plane attack on Cologne on 30 May. From 1943–1945, Germany was bombed almost every day.

Dam busters
In May 1943, British Lancaster bombers set off to destroy dams in Germany's Ruhr valleys. The planes carried "bouncing bombs", made to skip across a dam's reservoir and smash into the dam wall. Water gushing out would then flood the German factories of the Ruhr.

DRESDEN

By February 1945, the Allies had sent thousands of heavy bombers to pound Germany, almost unchallenged. Until 13 February, Dresden, an old city in the east, had escaped attack. That night, nearly 800 RAF bombers flew in. The next day, US bombers arriving to finish the attack witnessed the complete devastation of the city.

66 Even the tar on the roads melted. 99

FIRESTORM

Bombs started fires in Dresden and the old buildings burned easily. The fires merged into one huge blaze, sucking in storm-force winds that howled towards the inferno. Smoke rose high above a city now strewn with dead bodies.

Blazing city
After the bombers flew away, the once-beautiful medieval city of Dresden lay in ruins. The fire was seen 150 km (93 miles) away.

FAST FACTS

⊕ The bombing of Dresden was one of the most controversial actions of the war. Critics called it "terror bombing".

⊕ Nobody knows how many people died in Dresden. Some say probably around 25,000.

⊕ RAF bomber chief Arthur Harris claimed that bombing Dresden and other cities shortened the war.

BATTLE FOR BERLIN

By spring 1945, Hitler's Nazi empire lay in ruins, crushed between two vast armies. The Americans and their Allies were attacking from the west; Soviet forces from the east. Seven million Soviet soldiers poured across eastern Germany, heading for Berlin. Millions of German refugees fled west to escape them.

> **" ... the armies will do their duty.... "**
> Adolf Hitler

BERLIN IN FLAMES
Soviet troops encircled the city and fought their way in, street by street. Trapped in an underground bunker in the centre of the city, on 30 April, Hitler chose death rather than capture. Germany's military leaders then surrendered.

Losing battle
Soviet troops battled into Berlin. "Everyone hangs out a white flag", a Soviet soldier wrote home. There was little hope on one side, and little mercy on the other.

FAST FACTS

⊕ The battle for Berlin lasted from 16 April to 2 May 1945.

⊕ There were 2 million Soviet soldiers and 750,000 German soldiers in the city.

⊕ The fighting was fierce and at least 100,000 Russian soldiers were killed.

VICTORY IN EUROPE

Although still fighting the Soviets, the German army began surrendering to the western Allies. US General Eisenhower cabled to Washington and the world: "The mission of the Allied force was fulfilled at 02.41, local time, 7 May 1945".

FAST FACTS

 In Berlin, Field Marshal Keitl signed Germany's surrender. Russian generals partied all night long.

 In Britain, 8 and 9 May were public holidays, with flags, street parties, bonfires, and fireworks.

 Although the Pacific war with Japan continued, in New York there were parades, cheers, and speeches.

CELEBRATION

On 8 May 1945, crowds in Europe and the USA celebrated "Victory in Europe" (VE Day). This was made the official date, with the peace starting at one minute past midnight on 9 May. Soviet leader Stalin was furious, saying his troops were still fighting.

Joy on the streets
People celebrated on the streets of London (below), and in cities across Europe. But after victory, ruined Europe had to be rebuilt.

THE BATTLE OF THE ATLANTIC

The convoy battles of the North Atlantic were vital to keep the Allies fighting. Britain needed supplies from the US and Commonwealth allies such as Australia. Cargo ships carried food, oil, fuel, tanks, planes, guns, and clothing. But the ships were slow, and easy prey for warships, especially submarines. Losing the sea battle could mean losing the war.

SINKING THE BISMARCK

Germany could not risk sea battle with the powerful British or American fleets. So its big ships hunted convoys alone, or in pairs. In its brief eight-month career, one battleship would cause havoc. On 24 May 1941, Bismarck sank the British battlecruiser Hood – the pride of the Royal Navy. More than 1,400 crew died.

FAST FACTS

- Bismarck was named after Chancellor Otto Von Bismarck, who oversaw the unification of Germany in 1871.

- Bismarck and her sister ship Tirpitz were the largest battleships Germany built.

- Bismarck's eight 380-mm (15-in) guns fired shells that blew up HMS Hood. The ship sank in three minutes.

HUNT AND KILL

The British hunted down the Bismarck. Aircraft spotted it on 26 May, heading towards occupied France for safe haven, and torpedo planes from the carrier Ark Royal attacked. British warships closed in on the damaged and trapped Bismarck. Guns and torpedoes sank the biggest warship of the Nazi fleet on 27 May. Just 114 of more than 2,000 crew were saved.

Atlantic raider
Teamed with heavy cruiser Prinz Eugen, Bismarck was sent into the Atlantic to attack Allied convoys. Bismarck's top speed was 30 knots (56 kph/35 mph) – 52,000 tonnes of steel at full pelt.

Forward turret with two 380-mm (15-in) guns

Overall length was 251 m (823 ft)

Ship's command and control centre

Aft mast with radio and radar

CONVOY PQ 17

Merchant ships carrying cargo sailed in groups, or convoys, with warship guards. Yet even convoys were not safe from German submarines and planes. In July 1942, a convoy of 35 ships, code-named PQ 17, came under attack while sailing from Iceland with vital supplies for Russia.

FAST FACTS

 Convoy escorts included small ships such as destroyers, corvettes, and minesweepers.

 Larger Allied warships first escorted PQ 17 but were ordered back, in case the battleship Tirpitz appeared.

⊕ Nine U-boats and 39 planes joined in the attacks on PQ 17.

Under attack
The convoy was relentlessly bombed by German planes. The ships were no match for the planes' speed and agility.

CONVOY SCATTER!

As PQ 17 sailed into Arctic waters, orders came for its ships to scatter. The German battleship Tirpitz was reported close by. Instead, lurking German U-boats and planes attacked, sinking 24 of the convoy's 35 ships. Sailors, often burned by blazing fuel, stood little chance in the freezing ocean.

U-BOAT HUNTER

Sonar (sound echoes), radio, and sightings from planes helped Allied warships find and chase German U-boats. British Navy Captain Frederic "Johnnie" Walker was an expert sub hunter. From 1941 to 1944, he led attacks on U-boats such as U-202 – a Type VII submarine that could match a warship's speed on the surface.

> **"The only thing that... really frightened me... was the U-boat peril."**
> Winston Churchill

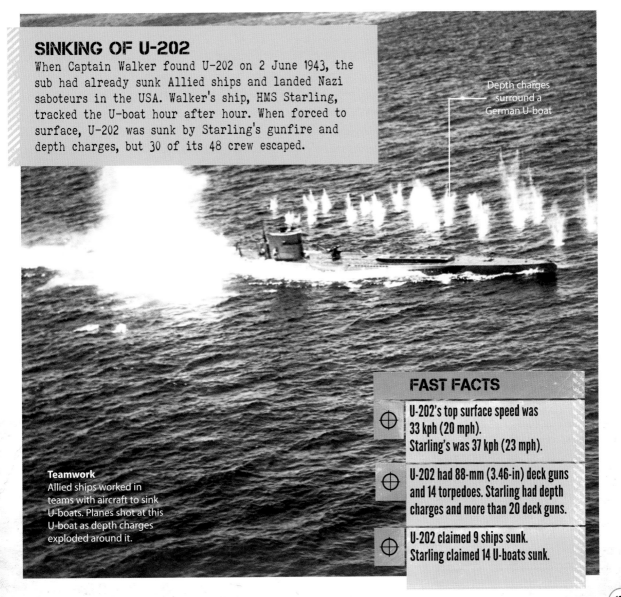

SINKING OF U-202

When Captain Walker found U-202 on 2 June 1943, the sub had already sunk Allied ships and landed Nazi saboteurs in the USA. Walker's ship, HMS Starling, tracked the U-boat hour after hour. When forced to surface, U-202 was sunk by Starling's gunfire and depth charges, but 30 of its 48 crew escaped.

Depth charges surround a German U-boat

Teamwork
Allied ships worked in teams with aircraft to sink U-boats. Planes shot at this U-boat as depth charges exploded around it.

FAST FACTS

⊕ U-202's top surface speed was 33 kph (20 mph). Starling's was 37 kph (23 mph).

⊕ U-202 had 88-mm (3.46-in) deck guns and 14 torpedoes. Starling had depth charges and more than 20 deck guns.

⊕ U-202 claimed 9 ships sunk. Starling claimed 14 U-boats sunk.

THE MEDITERRANEAN, BALKANS, AND MIDDLE EAST

Envious of Hitler's successes in Europe, Mussolini wanted victories himself. So in 1940 a new battle zone opened: the Mediterranean Sea, which was a vital trade route to the Balkan states of southeast Europe, North Africa, and the Middle East. Victories in these battles would gain the Axis sea routes, oilfields, new empires, and a southern base from which to attack Hitler's most hated enemy – Russia.

AXIS IN NORTH AFRICA

Mussolini began Italy's war in North Africa (September 1940) by sending troops from Libya to attack Egypt. Allied units under British General Wavell drove them back. An alarmed Hitler ordered German forces to help the Italians. The German desert tank army, the Afrika Korps, soon showed its worth.

FAST FACTS

⊕ The German Afrika Korps was an armoured force trained for desert war.

⊕ The Afrika Korps was commanded by the wily General Rommel.

⊕ The German air force flew in supplies from Sicily.

AFRIKA KORPS

As Allied forces fought an attack in the Balkans, Axis armies again swept east across the desert. Heading for Egypt, they retook Libya's important port of Tobruk. By the end of 1941, the Afrika Korps was ready to invade Egypt and take the vital Suez Canal.

British soldiers wore shorts in the heat of the Egyptian desert.

Fuel stop
In the desert war, speedy movement was the key to victory. Trucks and tanks filled up from fuel dumps spaced across hundreds of miles of desert.

A rifle is carried ready for action

LOAD NOT TO EXCEED 15-CWT

THE FALL OF CRETE

In October 1940, Italy invaded Greece. Tired of hearing about Hitler's victories in Europe, Mussolini wanted a success. Greece seemed a soft target, but the Greeks fought back. In April 1941, Hitler sent help and mainland Greece fell. Attention now turned to the Greek island of Crete.

> **❝ ... am not in the least anxious about airborne attack. ❞**
> **General Freyberg,**
> **Allied Commander, Crete**

FAST FACTS

⊕ The German attack on Crete was the first airborne invasion. It showed what paratroops – and surprise – could do.

⊕ More than 300 German transport planes were destroyed or damaged – a blow to Hitler's plans for new attacks.

⊕ 18,000 Allied soldiers were saved by the Royal Navy, but 9,000 fell prisoner to Germany.

ATTACK FROM THE SKIES

Allied troops from Greece had retreated to Crete, but expected the Germans. However, the scale of the attack by paratroopers took them by surprise. Despite fierce resistance, Germany took control of Crete over the next 10 days.

Silent warning
Code-breakers had warned of German invasion plans, but the Allies did not anticipate such a big airborne attack on Crete.

OPERATION RETRIBUTION

Yugoslavia had agreed to help the Axis powers. Then, in March 1941, its pro-Nazi government was thrown out by military leaders. Enraged, Hitler ordered Operation Retribution. German armies stormed into Yugoslavia.

FAST FACTS

⊕ Yugoslavia was an example of quick victory by "blitzkrieg" – troops on the ground and planes above.

⊕ Swift conquests of Yugoslavia and Greece were followed by a much bigger invasion – of Russia.

⊕ Yugoslav Resistance was split between the Serb Chetniks under Draza Mihailovic and the Communists under Josip Broz (Tito).

Bombed out
The Ju-87 Stuka plane bombed in a steep dive, its siren wailing to add to the terror of the attack.

STUKA STORM

Yugoslavs were no match for the German invaders, or their hordes of Stuka dive-bombers and other war planes. The short battle ended on 17 April 1941 with a Yugoslav surrender. Resistance fighters took to the mountains. They began a guerrilla war against the Nazis and each other.

TOBRUK

Tobruk was an Italian-held port of Libya. It rarely left the news in 1941 and 1942, as Axis and Allies fought for it during the North African desert war. When the Allies took Tobruk from the Italians in 1941, the "Desert Fox" - German General Rommel - determined to take it back.

FAST FACTS

 Italian troops held Tobruk because Libya had been an Italian colony since 1912.

 Allied soldiers at Tobruk called their own general "Ming the Merciless", after a comic-book villain.

 Both sides picked up enemy desert kit. Rommel wore British tank goggles over his Afrika Korps cap.

A solder drinks water to replace water loss in the heat

Tank personnel wore protective goggles

Radio headset for communication

DESERT FOX VERSUS DESERT RATS

Allied troops in North Africa called themselves the "Desert Rats". They held out in Tobruk for eight months until December 1941, when Rommel (the "Desert Fox") was pushed back. Then in June 1942, the Germans took the port, only for the British to get it back in November.

Feel the heat
Desert war was tough. Both sides ran out of fuel and supplies, and suffered heat that soared to 50°C (122°F).

ALAMEIN VICTORY

Rommel's Afrika Korps kept on attacking, heading for Egypt. In July 1942, General Auchinleck's 8th Army halted Rommel at El Alamein. Yet Churchill was not satisfied. He sent out a new general, Montgomery (nicknamed Monty), who finally gave the British public the desert victory they wanted.

FAST FACTS

⊕ Long Range Desert Group soldiers made patrols in trucks, roaming the desert to harass the enemy.

⊕ By October 1942, Rommel had only 200 battle tanks left, many of them old and needing repair.

⊕ Monty gathered more than 1,000 tanks, 1,500 aircraft, and hundreds of guns, to begin the battle.

MONTY'S TAKEOVER

Monty waited for more troops, planes, and tanks, including 250 US Shermans. With the second battle of El Alamein (October–November 1942), Monty won the victory Churchill had hoped for. At last, Rommel and his men were on the run across the desert.

Monty's black Royal Tank Regiment beret was loaned to him by his tank driver

Binoculars for observing the enemy

Leading from the front
Montgomery's command vehicle was an adapted M3 Grant tank nicknamed "Monty's charger".

BATTLE OF TARANTO

The British had to defeat Mussolini's navy to stop the dictator making the Mediterranean "Italy's Sea". In November 1940, they attacked the Italian naval base of Taranto. It crippled the Italian navy and showed how aircraft, even slow biplanes such as the Swordfish, could sink and damage warships.

Swordfish biplane on the flight deck of Illustrious

FAST FACTS

Twenty-one Swordfish biplanes were sent into the skies over Taranto on 11 November.

A Swordfish's top speed was 230 kph (143 mph). Torpedoes were dropped 900 m (0.5 mile) from the target.

The aircraft carrier HMS Illustrious had room for about 50 Swordfish-sized planes.

Slow but deadly
The British struck at night with Swordfish biplanes sent from the aircraft carrier Illustrious. Skimming low at 5.5 m (18 ft), the planes dropped torpedoes into the water.

SWORDFISH STRIKE

Swordfish torpedo bombers heavily damaged three Italian battleships on the night of 11 November, including the giant Littorio. It was the first ship-to-ship battle using aircraft, and was very effective.

MALTA UNDER SIEGE

The Mediterranean island of Malta was a British naval base between Europe and North Africa. From 1940 to 1942, Axis aircraft attacked it daily. Planes, ships, and U-boats hit convoys of ships carrying food, fuel, and weapons to the island.

FAST FACTS

- Thirty one Allied ships were sunk trying to reach Malta with supplies between 1940 and 1942.

- During the siege (11 June 1940– 20 November 1942), 1,493 civilians died and 3,674 were wounded.

- The RAF Gladiator biplane fighters that helped to defend Malta were named Faith, Hope, and Charity.

BATTLING THROUGH

Ships steaming to Malta came under ferocious attack. At first, the island had little air defence, just some old biplane fighters. Faster Hurricanes and Spitfires were brought in by sea to fight off German and Italian bombers.

Shops, homes, and churches were all hit

Children walk down a bombed-out street in Malta.

Raided
The Maltese people endured more than 3,000 air raids in little over two years.

OPERATION TORCH

Operation Torch was the first large amphibious invasion of WWII. Led by US General Eisenhower, it aimed to drive the Axis out of North Africa. On 8 November 1942, Allied forces landed in French-ruled Algeria and Morocco. US Army troops, supported by British forces, went into battle against the Germans for the first time.

Landing craft carried US troops to the beach

Beach parties landed first to organize supplies

Ocean operation
One invasion fleet sailed from the US and two from Britain. Sailors then reached the shore by landing craft.

AIR SUPPORT

American bombers flew raids on Axis bases in Tunisia and Sicily. The Allied landings in North Africa were supported by fighter aircraft, while transport planes flew in supplies to troops on the ground.

Sailors took the craft ashore

> **" ... an undertaking of a quite desperate nature... "**
> US General Eisenhower before Operation Torch landings

FAST FACTS

⊕ After landing, the Allies pushed east across North Africa.

⊕ The Allies had about 100,000 men in North Africa; the Axis had 60,000.

⊕ There were three landing sites for the US paratroopers: Casablanca, Oran, and Tangiers.

TAKING SICILY

After North Africa, the Allies targeted Italy. The Axis had been using Sicily as an air base to attack Allied ships. Invading Sicily would stop that, and be a stepping stone to Italy itself. Allied leaders believed the Italians were too war-weary to put up a fight. Landings in Sicily (Operation Husky) began in July 1943.

FAST FACTS

 Italian troops numbered 200,000; German troops numbered 50,000 or more.

 The Allies landed 160,000 men on the island of Sicily.

 There were more than 160,000 Axis casualties. The Allies suffered around 25,000 casualties.

American tank enters the city of Palermo in 1943

Welcome!
After the surrender, Allied troops were welcomed in Sicily.

BATTLE FOR SICILY

German troops proved readier to resist than the Italians and fighting in Sicily lasted 39 days, until 17 August. By then Mussolini had been ousted and Italy had begun secret peace talks. Hitler ordered German forces into Italy, to fight on after the Italian surrender on 3 September 1943.

ITALY INVADED

When Mussolini lost power in July 1943 the Allies hoped Italy would be an easy target. They were wrong. On 3 September, the Allies invaded mainland Italy but were resisted by the Germans. By 1 October, they had reached Naples. There they stopped, thwarted by bad weather, mountains, and German troops.

FAST FACTS

 Most Italians welcomed the Allies as "liberators".

 40,000 Allied troops landed on the beaches at Anzio.

The capture of Monte Cassino resulted in 55,000 Allied casualties.

FROM THE MOUNTAINS TO ROME

On 22 January 1944, during Operation Shingle, the Allies made a seaborne landing at Anzio, south of Rome. Troops then battled for every hill and village, bombarding the ancient abbey of Monte Cassino. Polish troops captured it on 18 May 1944, but Allied soldiers did not march into Rome until 4 June.

Bofors anti-aircraft gun

Gunners wore hard hats, but had no ear protection against noise

Battle for Monte Cassino
Allied anti-aircraft gunners had to stay alert. German planes were still around, looking for targets as the Allies fought through Italy.

Ammunition box

THE PACIFIC AND ASIA

WWII became truly global from 1941. As Japan made a bid to impose its rule on the Pacific, fighting spread from India to China, through southeast Asia towards Australia, and over vast stretches of the Pacific Ocean. Troops battled in jungle so dense men could scarcely hack trails, and fought for islands so small it seemed impossible for planes to land there.

JAPAN ATTACKS

Japan alarmed the US and Britain in the 1930s as its leaders grew friendly with the Nazis in Germany. Then, in 1937, Japan invaded China, where its air force bombed cities such as Nanking and Shanghai. Thousands of civilians were killed. Reports of Japanese cruelty and massacres shocked the world.

FAST FACTS

⊕ In 1931–1932 Japan occupied Manchuria (a region of northeast Asia, part of Russia and China).

⊕ In 1937, Japan attacked China. Chinese troops defended Shanghai for three months against 200,000 soldiers.

⊕ At least 200,000 Chinese died in a massacre at Nanking, December 1937–January 1938.

SPREADING POWER

The US protested against Japanese aggression in China. When Japanese troops moved into French Indo-China (Laos and Vietnam), America banned oil and metal supplies to Japan. The Japanese government now saw the Americans as their main enemy. Hideji Tojo became prime minister in October 1941 and prepared for war with the US.

Japan on the march
Japanese troops took over Manchuria and much of China. The Chinese fought desperately as better-armed Japanese armies destroyed their cities and villages.

PEARL HARBOR

The US Pacific naval base at Pearl Harbor, on Oahu island, Hawaii, was home to the US Pacific fleet. Europe was at war, but the Pacific remained at peace, and Japanese "peace envoys" were in Washington. But overnight, a Japanese naval force steamed into position, 320 km (200 miles) north of Oahu. As dawn broke on Sunday 7 December 1941, the Japanese launched a surprise attack on Pearl Harbor. The next day, the US declared war on Japan.

USS California is hit and lists (leans) as it begins to sink

❝ ... the USA was suddenly and deliberately attacked by naval and air forces of the Empire of Japan. ❞
US President Roosevelt

The crew abandon their burning ship

DAY OF INFAMY

The Japanese strike force had six carrier ships and more than 300 aircraft. Its three "midget" submarines were sunk, but the air attack was successful. Four out of eight US battleships were sunk, 21 ships were wrecked or damaged, and 300 aircraft were destroyed. But the dockyard and fuel tanks were not badly hit, and two carriers, 13 cruisers, and 24 destroyers were out at sea.

Under fire
Defenders of Pearl Harbor fought gallantly amid smoke, flames, and confusion as Japanese bombs and torpedoes struck their ships.

FAST FACTS

⊕ The first bombs at Pearl Harbor fell at 07.55 am.

⊕ There were 92 US ships at Pearl Harbor when the Japanese attacked.

⊕ US casualties numbered 3,303 killed or missing and 1,272 wounded.

SINGAPORE FALLS

The Japanese had taken Hong Kong, Thailand, Guam, and Wake Island by Christmas 1941. Then they moved into Thailand and Malaya, aiming to capture the British base on Singapore. Britain was sure attack could come only from the sea, but a Japanese raid through the jungles of Malaya took Singapore by surprise.

FAST FACTS

⊕ Japanese troops moved into Thailand on 9 December 1941.

⊕ On 10 December, the Japanese sank the British warships HMS Prince of Wales and HMS Repulse.

⊕ On 15 February 1942, the British commander of Singapore surrendered.

Bayonet blades were attached to rifles

An advancing Japanese soldier keeps low to the ground

Fight to the end
Japanese soldiers believed they must win, or die. Here, infantry are fighting in Singapore in 1942.

SURRENDER OR DIE

After the surrender of Singapore in February 1942, captured British, Australian, and Indian soldiers were badly treated by the Japanese, who believed that surrender was cowardly.

BATAAN

Early in December 1941, Japan landed troops in the Philippines. US and Filipino forces there were led by General MacArthur, who strategically fell back as Japan took Manila, the capital. The forces were left to defend a few strongholds on the Bataan Peninsula and Corregidor Island. They fought for three months at Bataan, but were defeated and surrendered in April 1942.

FAST FACTS

⊕ Manila fell to the Japanese on 2 January 1942.

⊕ The Battle of Bataan lasted three months, from 7 January to 9 April 1942.

⊕ The surrender at Bataan is the largest surrender in American and Filipino history.

A Japanese soldier rounds up US and Filipino troops

Losing battle
The Japanese at Bataan could replace men who fell sick, were wounded, or killed. The Americans could not. More men died from sickness than in battle.

DEATH MARCH

After surrendering at Bataan, survivors taken prisoner were forced to march to a prison camp. Many people died on the "Bataan Death March". Corregidor Island also fell after a fierce battle, and by May, Japan had taken over the Philippines.

123

MILNE BAY

In 1942, Japan planned to seize New Guinea and Midway Island, to set up bases from which to attack Allied ships. But in New Guinea, Australian and US infantry fought Japanese landing from the sea. At the Battle of Milne Bay, Japan's forces met stiff Allied resistance – and their first defeat.

FAST FACTS

⊕ The Battle of Milne Bay, New Guinea, lasted two weeks from 25 August to 7 September 1942.

⊕ There were more than four times as many Australian and American troops as Japanese.

⊕ Japanese snipers tied themselves to treetops to shoot at Allied soldiers. Some Japanese "played dead", then got up and fired.

JUNGLE WAR

Fighting on islands such as Java, New Guinea, and New Britain in 1942–1943, Allied troops quickly learned about jungle war. The dense mountain jungle on the islands meant soldiers often did not know where their enemy was.

> " ... it was the Australians who first broke the invincibility of the Japanese army. "
> Field Marshal Slim

Bush hats kept off sun and rain. Insects were much harder to repel.

Mosquito attack
Allied troops at Milne Bay were attacked by malaria-carrying mosquitoes as well as the enemy. Many men fell ill because they had no protective mosquito nets.

DOOLITTLE RAID

The Japanese believed their homeland was beyond enemy reach. However, in April 1942, US aircraft carriers USS Enterprise and USS Hornet (which the Japanese missed at Pearl Harbor) went to sea with 16 B-25 bombers, 80 airmen, and Colonel James Doolittle of the US Army Corps. Doolittle led the first US bomber raid on Japan.

FAST FACTS

⊕ The US B-25 bombers carried four 27-kg (500-lb) bombs.

⊕ The Doolittle planes had dummy tail guns to deter Japanese attacks from the rear.

⊕ A B-25 had a crew of five: pilot, co-pilot, navigator, gunner, and radio operator.

Takeoff
A Doolittle B-25 takes off from USS Hornet. Fifteen planes got to China and one landed in Russia. None of the planes got home, but all but three of the crew survived.

B-25 takes off from the flight deck

Carrier flight deck crew

66 Our destination is Tokyo. 99
Colonel James Doolittle

TOKYO TARGETED!

The B-25s took off 1,050 km (650 miles) from their target, flying low to avoid being spotted. Six hours after launch, they bombed Tokyo. Doolittle's planes could not land back on the carriers, but flew on to China. The raids did little damage, but shocked Japan's government.

MIDWAY

In May 1942, a big Japanese fleet attacked Port Moresby in New Guinea. They were beaten by Allied warships at the Battle of the Coral Sea. Japan then sent most of its fleet against the US base on Midway Island, not knowing that there were three US aircraft carriers nearby. The battle that followed resulted in an important win for the Allies.

FAST FACTS

 The Battle of Midway lasted three days, from 4 to 7 June 1942.

 Allied code-breakers discovered the Japanese plan to attack Midway. This allowed them to plan a defence.

 The US carriers had 233 aircraft; the Japanese had about 250, but they were widely distributed.

CRUNCH BATTLE

As the Japanese attacked, US planes roared in. The US Navy bombed and torpedoed three Japanese aircraft carriers. Japanese planes hit back to sink the carrier USS Yorktown, but then their own carrier Hiryu was sunk. By the end of the battle, US planes had sunk four Japanese carriers.

USS Yorktown is struck by a bomb at the Battle of Midway

Morale booster
Warships came under air attack at Midway. Sinking four Japanese aircraft carriers was an important victory for the US Pacific fleet.

GUADALCANAL

One of the Pacific's fiercest battles was at Guadalcanal in the Solomon Islands. In July 1942, Japanese soldiers arrived to build an airstrip for a possible strike against Australia. On 8 August 1942, 19,000 US Marines landed to stop them.

ISLAND STRUGGLE

By October, 45,000 troops were fighting in a battle that swayed this way and that, as the Japanese landed more troops and the Americans held them off. But, in February 1943, the Japanese gave up and quit Guadalcanal.

FAST FACTS

⊕ There were more than 25,000 Japanese losses, including 9,000 deaths from disease.

⊕ Crocodiles gathered to feed on Japanese bodies lying on the beach.

⊕ The Marines nicknamed one Japanese plane "Washing Machine Charlie" because of the noise it made.

Protected airfield
US Marines renamed the Japanese airfield Henderson Field, and defended it fiercely.

SAIPAN

The Allies island-hopped across the Pacific from 1943, flushing out the Japanese to win back island groups such as the Marianas. A key battle took place for Saipan Island, where US Marines took on 30,000 Japanese troops in a campaign that lasted almost a month.

THE TURKEY SHOOT

At sea, Japanese forces took a bad defeat, losing six aircraft carriers. In the air, 300 Japanese planes were destroyed on 19 June, compared to 16 US losses. It became known as the "Great Marianas Turkey Shoot".

FAST FACTS

 The battle for Saipan lasted from 15 June to 9 July 1944.

 US Navy pilot David McCampbell shot down seven Japanese planes in two sorties.

 Japan's leader Tojo resigned in shame at the defeat.

Heading for land
US Marines rode ashore at Saipan in an amphibious landing craft that could travel on land as well as water.

Military police controlled beach traffic

PORTLAND ROSE

7015800 USA S

LEYTE GULF

During 1944, Allied forces moved closer to regaining the Philippines. They planned first to take the island of Leyte. Knowing the Japanese would fight hard, the Allies built up a huge landing force of 750 ships to invade on 20 October 1944. It would become the biggest naval battle in history.

Water borne
Most planes needed a carrier ship or airstrip to land on, but seaplanes, such as this American scout plane, had floats to land on the water.

Filling the fuel tank through the aircraft's wing

KAMIKAZE CRASHES
Sailors on US warships in Leyte Gulf had their first sight of Japanese kamikaze (suicide pilots), who deliberately crashed their planes into Allied ships.

FAST FACTS

⊕ The Japanese lost four aircraft carriers, 10 cruisers, and three battleships, including their biggest ship, the Musashi.

⊕ Musashi sank after hits from 19 torpedoes, and as many bombs.

⊕ The US fleet lost just three small escort carriers.

IWO JIMA

By the start of 1945 the US needed a new base from which to launch air raids against Japan. They picked Iwo Jima ("Sulphur island"). The resulting battle between the US Marines and the Japanese on the island was one of the bloodiest battles of the war, but by April the airstrip was ready.

FAST FACTS

 US Marines landed on Iwo Jima on 15 February 1945. Fighting did not end until 16 March.

 Marines raised the Stars and Stripes (US flag) on Mt Suribachi on 23 February.

 Iwo Jima is just 8 km (5 miles) long.

DEATH ISLAND

The 20,000 Japanese on Iwo Jima had dug into its hills, sheltering in caves and bunkers. The battle saw nearly every Japanese defender killed, and also 6,000 Marines. Despite US troops suffering higher casualties (in terms of troops injured) than the Japanese, they won the battle.

" We hated them… but we did respect their ability. "
Lt Caruso
(US Marines)

The Marines landed after heavy bombardment of the island from air and sea

OKINAWA

The Japanese had promised to fight to the end for their homeland, and the last "stepping stone" to the main islands of Japan was Okinawa. Allied troops landed there on 26 March 1945. They faced a desperate battle, one the Japanese called "the rain of steel".

FAST FACTS

- The huge Allied fleet included 37 aircraft carriers and 19 battleships.
- Admiral Raymond Spruance of the US Navy led the attack.
- Allied casualties included about 12,000 killed and 36,000 wounded.

Crash and burn
Gunners on Allied warships fired at Japanese pilots, knowing that some were kamikaze (suicide fliers) aiming to crash onto the ship.

RAIN OF STEEL

The battle for Okinawa lasted 82 days. By the time it ended on 21 June 1945, the Allies had lost 30 ships, with many more damaged in suicide attacks by Japanese kamikaze pilots. On the island itself, more than 100,000 Japanese died.

THE ATOMIC BOMB

By June 1945, war in Europe was over. The Allies had also liberated Burma and Borneo. Daily air raids pounded Japan. Still the Japanese fought on. Allied leaders feared they would have to invade Japan for a terrible last battle. Then came news that US scientists had tested the "ultimate weapon": the first atomic bomb.

Instant death
The bomb was dropped on the city of Hiroshima. Of its 343,000 inhabitants, 60,000 died at once. Many more died later.

A mushroom cloud rose more than 18,000 m (60,000 ft) above Hiroshima in just 10 minutes

A cloud of thick, black smoke engulfed the devastated city below

ULTIMATE DESTRUCTION

President Truman gave the go-ahead, and on 6 August 1945 a US B-29 bomber dropped an atomic bomb over the Japanese city of Hiroshima. On 9 August a second bomb was dropped on Nagasaki. Both cities were almost wiped from the map.

FAST FACTS

⊕ The B-29 that dropped the Hiroshima bomb was called Enola Gay.

⊕ Enola Gay's captain was Colonel Paul Tibbets Jr.

⊕ Each bomb was named. Hiroshima's was "Little Boy"; Nagasaki's was "Fat Man".

THE WAR ENDS

On 8 August 1945, between the two atomic bombs, the Russians attacked Japan. Emperor Hirohito decided Japan must stop fighting, or be destroyed. On 2 September, the Japanese met Allied leaders on the US battleship Missouri in Tokyo Bay and signed the surrender. The Pacific war was over, and so was World War II.

FAST FACTS

- The death toll from the bombs is estimated at 135,000, though the real figure will never be known.

- 2 September became known as "Victory over Japan" (VJ) day.

- Some Japanese soldiers would not surrender and lived in Pacific island jungles for up to 30 years.

ATOMIC AGE

After the bombs were dropped on Hiroshima and Nagasaki, the cities were almost totally lifeless. No one had ever seen destruction caused by humans on such a scale before. The world had entered a terrifying new chapter - the atomic age.

The aftermath
In Hiroshima, nearly every building within 1.6 km (1 mile) of the explosion point was destroyed.

CHAPTER FOUR: TECHNOLOGY of WAR

World War II was a war of science and technology. An awesome array of hi-tech weapons went to war, from tanks to rockets and super-bombs. Technology gave the military new tools for defence and attack, such as radar, sonar, coding machines, and computers to "crack" machine codes. Battlefield soldiers now fought with weapons invented by scientists and engineers – the "backroom" brains behind new technology.

"My God, what have we done?"

Captain Robert A Lewis,
on dropping the atomic bomb on Hiroshima

IN THIS CHAPTER:

TANKS

Tanks fought in every war zone in WWII, with huge tank battles in Russia, western Europe, and North Africa. Armies had "heavy" tanks that were very slow, and "light" tanks that were more like armoured cars. Old-fashioned generals used tanks to follow infantry into battle or as big guns on wheels. Only far-thinking planners realised that tanks could win battles - and perhaps even win the war.

GERMAN PANTHER

Germany's Panther D (1943) was the best all-round tank of WWII. The German army took up all the latest ideas about tanks, and used them in a new and effective way. New tanks like the Panther soon ruled the battlefield, while the Allies rushed to get bigger tanks of their own into battle.

SPECIFICATIONS

Size 6.9 m (22 ft 6 in) | 3 m (9 ft 10 in)

Crew 5

Speed 45 kph (28 mph)

Arms 1 x 75 mm (3 in) gun, plus 2 machine guns

BIG CAT

The Panther was designed to be simpler and cheaper than the Tiger, Germany's most advanced tank. It was impressive, but its new drive system broke down too often. It was easier to make than the Tiger, though, and about 6,000 were built.

Muzzle brake to reduce "recoil", which made the gun barrel shake

Long-barrelled 75 mm (3 in) gun

Big Cat
The Panther weighed 44.7 tonnes and had front armour 140 mm (5.5 in) thick.

New drive system linked to wheels and tank tracks

GERMAN PZKW III

In Poland, 1939, and France, 1940, the German PzKw III tank proved too fast and powerful for its rivals. The tanks attacked in wedge (arrow) formation. Commanders led the armies, giving orders by radio.

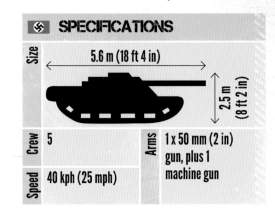

SPECIFICATIONS

Size	5.6 m (18 ft 4 in) / 2.5 m (8 ft 2 in)
Crew	5
Speed	40 kph (25 mph)
Arms	1 x 50 mm (2 in) gun, plus 1 machine gun

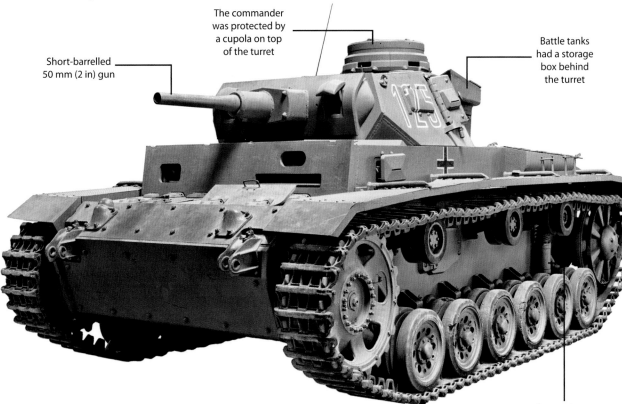

The commander was protected by a cupola on top of the turret

Short-barrelled 50 mm (2 in) gun

Battle tanks had a storage box behind the turret

Suspension system to ease the jolts and bumps

DESIGN AND DEVELOPMENT

Nazi Germany built its first tanks secretly in the 1930s. The PzKw III was developed from small light tanks, such as the 10-tonne PzKw II. It had a much better gun and armour, and fought in many battles until replaced in the front line by the PzKw IV and Panther.

Team tank
A tank crew went into battle as a team. The PzKw III had a crew of five: commander, gunner, loader, driver, and radio operator/gunner. The driver looked out through optical equipment at the front.

BRITISH MATILDA II

The Matilda II was Britain's best tank when the war began. Its steel armour was thick enough to withstand most guns, but its own "2-pounder" gun was not very powerful. Matilda II did well in Europe and North Africa until better Allied tanks came into service in 1942.

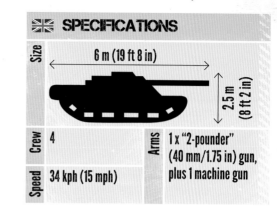

🇬🇧 SPECIFICATIONS

Size	6 m (19 ft 8 in) wide, 2.5 m (8 ft 2 in) high		
Crew	4	**Arms**	1 x "2-pounder" (40 mm/1.75 in) gun, plus 1 machine gun
Speed	34 kph (15 mph)		

Keep the tanks rolling
Wartime factories and workshops were kept busy building tanks and repairing damaged or broken-down tanks. Fitters replaced worn-out parts, and added new guns and armour protection.

DESIGN AND DEVELOPMENT

The British pioneered tanks in World War I (1914–1918). In the 1930s they adopted the ideas of US tank designer J Walter Christie, but in 1940, Britain still had only 200 modern tanks. Tank production had to be stepped up fast.

RUSSIAN T-34

From 1941, German armies fighting in Russia came to respect the Russian T-34 tanks, which battled them in large numbers. The first version of this tough fighting vehicle was the T-34/76. This was followed in 1943 by the more powerful T-34/85, which had a bigger gun with superior fire power.

SPECIFICATIONS

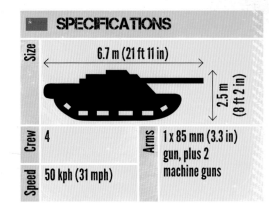

Size	6.7 m (21 ft 11 in) / 2.5 m (8 ft 2 in)
Crew	4
Speed	50 kph (31 mph)
Arms	1 x 85 mm (3.3 in) gun, plus 2 machine guns

85 mm (3.3 in) main gun

Driver's position at the front of the tank, beneath the main gun

BIG BROTHER

The T-34/85 became the standard Russian tank and was produced continually until the end of the war. By then, Russia had 22,000 T-34/85s compared with only 2,000 German Tigers.

Big gun, thick armour
The T-34/85 had an extra-large gun to take on the German Panthers. Its sloped armour was designed to protect the crew from enemy fire.

GERMAN TIGER

The 1941 Tiger I was Germany's answer to Russia's KV-1 and T-34. It was so fearsome that enemy tank crews often decided to back off when it was spotted. The Tiger's big gun could blow up a target at long range, while enemy shells either fell short or bounced off it.

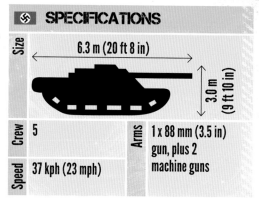

SPECIFICATIONS

Size	6.3 m (20 ft 8 in) · 3.0 m (9 ft 10 in)
Crew	5
Speed	37 kph (23 mph)
Arms	1 x 88 mm (3.5 in) gun, plus 2 machine guns

Main 88 mm (3.5 in) gun with a very long barrel, plus 92 rounds (shells)

Low turret, making it a hard target to hit

The Tiger had side steel armour almost as thick as its front armour

Heavy going
The Tiger was a fearsome monster, but it was very expensive. It was so heavy it often collapsed weak roads and bridges. It was designed to be able to "wade" through water up to 4 m (13 ft) deep.

DESIGN AND DEVELOPMENT
German engineers tried to make the Tiger unbeatable. Its front armour was 10 cm (4 in) thick, so most enemy guns could not penetrate it. Its weakness was its short range – only 112 km (70 miles). The even bigger 1944 Tiger II or "King Tiger" outclassed all Allied tanks.

US SHERMAN M4·A3

The US Sherman was the best all-round Allied tank of World War II. Nine upgrades were produced, including the M4A3 and the Firefly, which had the biggest guns. The Sherman's weakness was its tendency to catch fire easily when hit.

SPECIFICATIONS

Size	5.8 m (19 ft 1 in)	2.7 m (8 ft 10 in)
Crew	5	**Arms** 1 x 76.2 mm (3 in) gun, plus 2 machine guns
Speed	42 kph (26 mph)	

MASS PRODUCTION

The Sherman was designed to be simple, tough, and fast. More than 40,000 were built, and in the end it was sheer numbers that counted in a tank battle. The Allies made too many tanks too fast for the Germans to compete.

Long-barrelled 76.2 mm (3 in) gun

Soldiers' friend
Tank crews liked the Sherman. It was reliable and kept going. Improved versions such as the M4A3 and Firefly had bigger guns.

Rubber-padded track plates to reduce wear and tear

CHURCHILL "FUNNY"

The British Churchill tank (1940) was designed in a rush. It was too slow, and its turret was too small for the big gun it needed. It was mechanically complicated, and often broke down. Despite these problems, the Churchill did many useful jobs as one of the "funny" tanks used by the Allies on D-Day in 1944.

SPECIFICATIONS

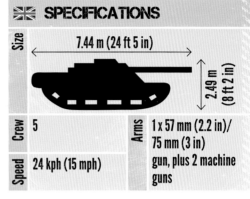

Size 7.44 m (24 ft 5 in)

2.49 m (8 ft 2 in)

Crew 5

Speed 24 kph (15 mph)

Arms 1 x 57 mm (2.2 in)/ 75 mm (3 in) gun, plus 2 machine guns

Bobbin mat unrolled from the spool on top of the tank

Bobbin along
The "bobbin" tank crawled up the beaches carrying a roll of canvas cloth matting. The mat was 3 m (10 ft) wide. As it unrolled, it made a track across the sand and mud for Allied vehicles.

FUNNY TANKS

Army engineers modified tanks to do other jobs, such as laying a bridge or clearing a minefield. This was the idea behind the "funnies" that helped the Allies land on the Normandy beaches on D-Day. There were swimming tanks, flame-throwing tanks, ditch-bridging tanks, and track-laying tanks, such as this Churchill "bobbin" tank.

Tank body with gun removed for "funny" modification

AIRCRAFT

When World War II began in 1939, air forces still had many slow, old-fashioned aircraft. Few of these planes outlasted the first battles. In 1944, jets and rocket planes hurtled into combat for the first time, taking the world into a new age of air warfare. By 1945, planes had seen action in war zones from the Arctic to the tropics.

DE HAVILLAND MOSQUITO

The British De Havilland Mosquito was a remarkable aircraft. It flew fast and high, as a night fighter or to take spy photos. It also flew very low, at treetop height, to bomb enemy targets with great accuracy. The Mosquito was - even more remarkably - made almost entirely of wood, to save precious metal alloys. It was built in Britain, Australia, and Canada.

⬛ SPECIFICATIONS

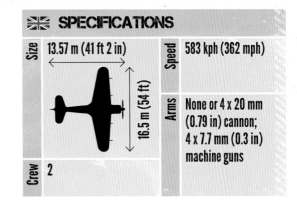

Size	13.57 m (41 ft 2 in) 16.5 m (54 ft)	**Speed**	583 kph (362 mph)
Crew	2	**Arms**	None or 4 x 20 mm (0.79 in) cannon; 4 x 7.7 mm (0.3 in) machine guns

PATHFINDERS

Mosquito planes flew as "pathfinders" to guide Allied bombers. They went on ahead of the main, slower bomber force to pinpoint the target with flares. Famous RAF pilots such as Leonard Cheshire VC flew Mosquitoes over Germany to "mark" targets.

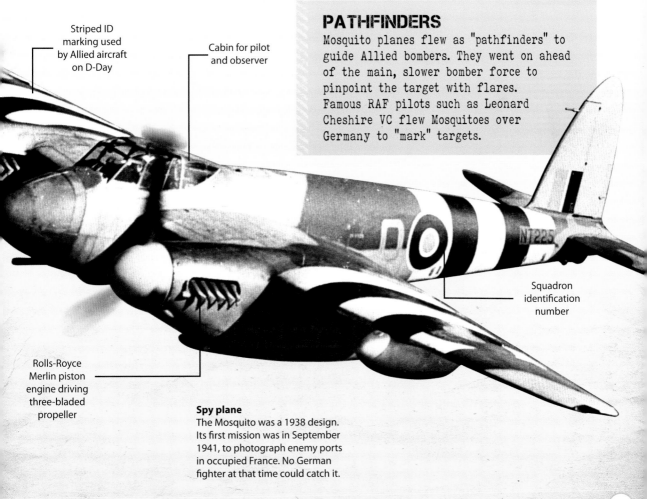

Striped ID marking used by Allied aircraft on D-Day

Cabin for pilot and observer

Squadron identification number

Rolls-Royce Merlin piston engine driving three-bladed propeller

Spy plane
The Mosquito was a 1938 design. Its first mission was in September 1941, to photograph enemy ports in occupied France. No German fighter at that time could catch it.

SPITFIRE

The Spitfire was the best-known British aircraft of the war. It fought in the Battle of Britain (1940) and flew in combat from Europe to the Pacific. This graceful, deadly aircraft was much loved by its pilots, who found it a joy to fly. The Spitfire remains an icon of World War II.

⌗ SPECIFICATIONS

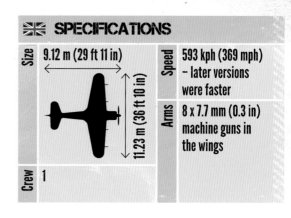

Size	9.12 m (29 ft 11 in) — 11.23 m (36 ft 10 in)	Speed	593 kph (369 mph) – later versions were faster
		Arms	8 x 7.7 mm (0.3 in) machine guns in the wings
Crew	1		

SUPER-SPIT

Designed by R J Mitchell, the Spitfire first flew in 1936 and was soon in RAF service. Improved marks, or types, of the Spitfire flew faster and higher. The Seafire, a naval type, flew from carriers.

It was able to climb to a height of almost 7,000 m (23,000 ft) in just over 9 minutes.

Thick "bullet proof" windshield to protect pilot from head-on attacks

Spitfire success
German pilots who first fought the Spitfire in 1940 demanded a plane like it. The British fighter had eight machine guns in the wings. Pilots liked to get close to the enemy before shooting.

The RAF roundel marks the aircraft as British

All-metal fuselage (body) of light alloy plates

MESSERSCHMITT ME-109

The Messerschmitt Me-109 was the Luftwaffe's main fighter plane. About 35,000 were built - more than any other warplane of World War II, after Russia's Sturmovik. Me-109s took part in all the air battles of the war in Europe, Russia, and North Africa - from the invasion of Poland in September 1939 to the fall of Berlin in April 1945.

⚙ SPECIFICATIONS

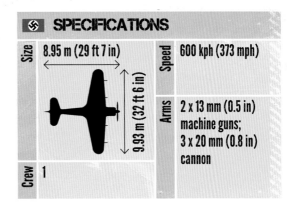

Size	8.95 m (29 ft 7 in) / 9.93 m (32 ft 6 in)	**Speed**	600 kph (373 mph)
Crew	1	**Arms**	2 x 13 mm (0.5 in) machine guns; 3 x 20 mm (0.8 in) cannon

Pilot's cockpit with armour protection

Flying escort
Me-109s often flew as escorts to German bombers. They stayed above and behind the main force, ready to pounce on Allied fighters trying to attack.

Machine guns or cannon in aircraft nose

Square-tipped, thin wings for speed

ACE FIGHTERS
The Messerschmitt Me-109 was the Spitfire's rival in many air battles. It first flew in 1935, and proved tough enough to fight all through the war. Almost every German ace pilot flew the Me-109 at some stage.

MITSUBISHI A6M ZERO

The Japanese Navy's Mitsubishi A6M Zero was Japan's most successful fighter aircraft. To Allied pilots, the sky above the blue Pacific seemed to be full of Zeros from 1941 to 1942. In the last years of the war, new Allied fighter planes outflew the Zero, but it was still fighting in 1945 when the war ended.

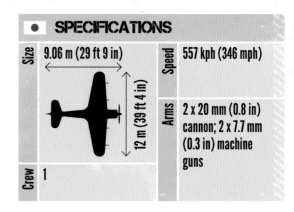

● SPECIFICATIONS

Size	9.06 m (29 ft 9 in) / 12 m (39 ft 4 in)	Speed	557 kph (346 mph)
		Arms	2 x 20 mm (0.8 in) cannon; 2 x 7.7 mm (0.3 in) machine guns
Crew	1		

Well armed
The Zero was fast, acrobatic, and popular with pilots. It was heavily armed, with two cannon in the wings and two machine guns in the fuselage body.

ZERO SHOCK

Reports had told the Allies that Japanese aircraft were poor, so when pilots first met the Zero in 1941, it came as a shock. The Zero could outclimb, out-turn, and outrun most US and British aircraft – but it met its match in the US Navy's F4U Corsair.

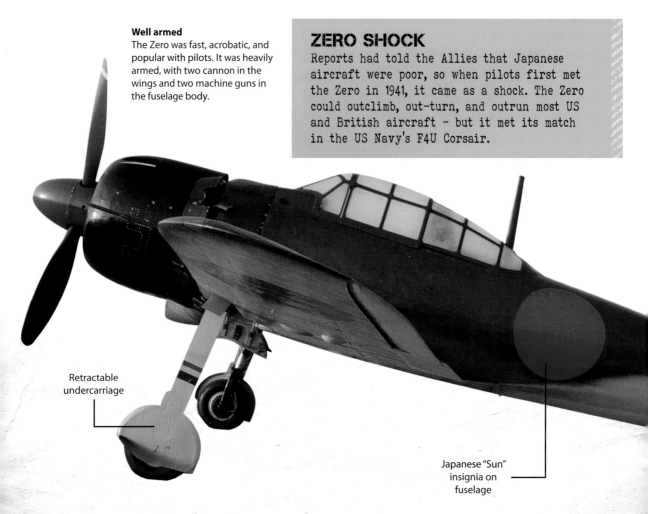

Retractable undercarriage

Japanese "Sun" insignia on fuselage

VOUGHT F4U CORSAIR

Japanese pilots in Pacific air battles found the F4U Corsair the best US Navy fighter. Like the Zero, the Corsair flew from carriers, but it was a much bigger aircraft, twice as heavy as the Zero fighter. The F4U could carry bombs as well as fight in air combat.

SPECIFICATIONS

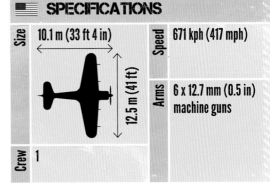

Size	10.1 m (33 ft 4 in) 12.5 m (41 ft)	Speed	671 kph (417 mph)
		Arms	6 x 12.7 mm (0.5 in) machine guns
Crew	1		

Bullet-proof glass was set behind the curved perspex windshield

Distinctive wings
The Corsair had an easy-to-spot, angled "gull-wing". Like most carrier aircraft, the Corsair's wings folded, for storing on board ship.

Space for two bombs beneath the fuselage

Star insignia carried on all US warplanes

61-120

PACIFIC PIRATE

The Corsair first saw combat with the US Marines at Guadalcanal in February 1943. It then joined both the US and British navies as a carrier strike plane. With six guns in the wings, plus a pair of 454 kg (1,000 lb) bombs, the Corsair was a hard-to-beat warplane for Pacific raiding.

LANCASTER BOMBER

The Avro Lancaster led RAF Bomber Command's night raids on Germany from 1942. This four-engined aircraft dropped a 9979-kg (22,000-lb) "grand slam" bomb, the heaviest carried by any World War II bomber.

SPECIFICATIONS

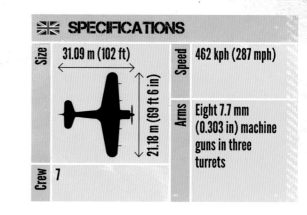

Size	31.09 m (102 ft)	**Speed**	462 kph (287 mph)
	21.18 m (69 ft 6 in)	**Arms**	Eight 7.7 mm (0.303 in) machine guns in three turrets
Crew	7		

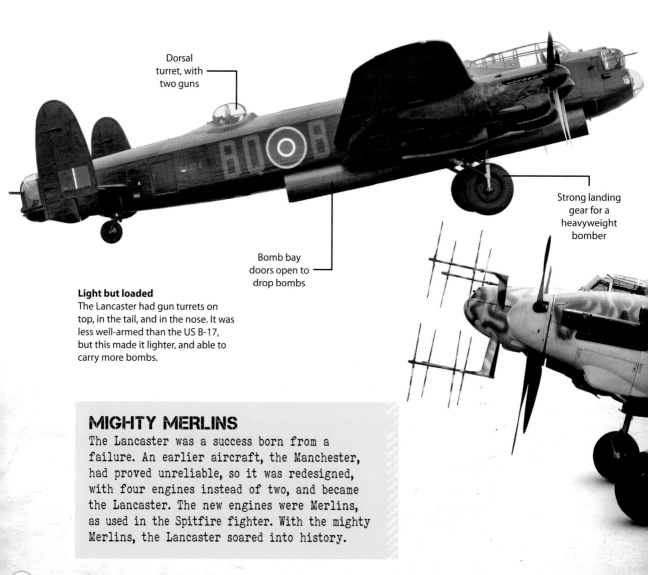

Dorsal turret, with two guns

Strong landing gear for a heavyweight bomber

Bomb bay doors open to drop bombs

Light but loaded
The Lancaster had gun turrets on top, in the tail, and in the nose. It was less well-armed than the US B-17, but this made it lighter, and able to carry more bombs.

MIGHTY MERLINS

The Lancaster was a success born from a failure. An earlier aircraft, the Manchester, had proved unreliable, so it was redesigned, with four engines instead of two, and became the Lancaster. The new engines were Merlins, as used in the Spitfire fighter. With the mighty Merlins, the Lancaster soared into history.

MESSERSCHMITT BF 110

Allied bombers, such as the Lancaster, expected attack from German night fighters such as the Messerschmitt Bf 110. This twin-engine fighter was too slow for air combat after 1940, but was adapted for night flying. At first, its crew had only their own eyes to spot bombers but by 1942, most night fighters had radar.

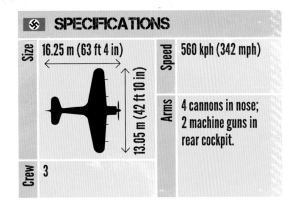

SPECIFICATIONS

Size	16.25 m (63 ft 4 in) / 13.05 m (42 ft 10 in)	**Speed**	560 kph (342 mph)
Crew	3	**Arms**	4 cannons in nose; 2 machine guns in rear cockpit.

The Bf 110 sneaked up on aircraft from beneath, with a gun that fired up into the belly of the Allied bomber plane.

NIGHT HUNTING

Ground control alerted Bf 110 night-fighter pilots, who flew into position to await Allied bombers. The aircraft's own radar was simple, but could pick up enemy raiders. Then the fighter closed in to shoot down the bomber with its powerful guns. The Allies found a way to fool a night fighter's radar, by using strips of metal foil to jam it.

Enemy detector
The Bf 110 night fighter hunted by radar, picking up signals with antenna in the aircraft's nose. The plane had powerful guns for its use as a "bomber-destroyer".

Under-wing rack for extra tanks or bombs

Tail wheel

Swastika emblem on tail

CATALINA

An Allied pilot shot down over the sea and floating in a dinghy would be happy to see a Catalina. This twin-engine US amphibious aircraft flew life-saving rescue missions. It could land on the sea, or drop a lifeboat carried under its wing to rescue men in the water.

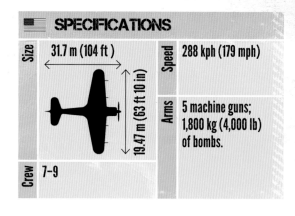

SPECIFICATIONS

Size	31.7 m (104 ft) 19.47 m (63 ft 10 in)	**Speed**	288 kph (179 mph)
		Arms	5 machine guns; 1,800 kg (4,000 lb) of bombs.
Crew	7-9		

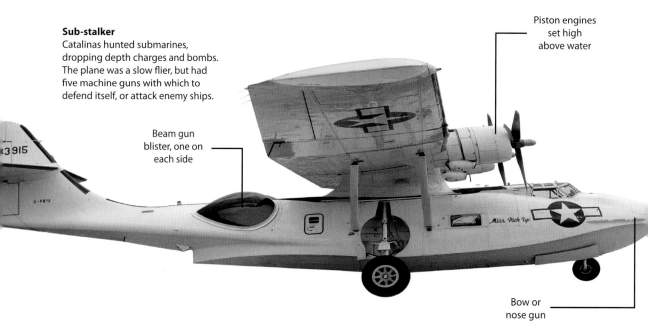

Sub-stalker
Catalinas hunted submarines, dropping depth charges and bombs. The plane was a slow flier, but had five machine guns with which to defend itself, or attack enemy ships.

Piston engines set high above water

Beam gun blister, one on each side

Bow or nose gun

OCEAN LIFE-SAVER

The Catalina joined the US Navy in 1936 and pilots from Allied nations flew it during World War II. The Catalina had a boat-shaped hull and twin floats under high wings. These allowed the plane to land on the sea. It also had wheels for dry-land landings and take-offs. This aircraft was at home on land or water, as well as in the air.

C-47 DAKOTA

The C-47 Dakota, or Skytrain, was World War II's most-used transport plane. It was a reliable "load-carrier", taking Allied troops into battle, dropping supplies in jungles, and flying wounded soldiers to hospital. Without the Dakota, the Allies might not have won the war.

SPECIFICATIONS

Size	29 m (95 ft) / 19.6 m (64 ft 5in)	**Speed**	250 kph (155 mph)
Crew	3	**Arms**	None; carried up to 3,200 kg (7,000 lb) load

ANYWHERE, ANYTIME

The C-47 Dakota was adapted from a reliable pre-war airliner, the DC-3. It was easy to give it a stronger cabin floor for heavier loads, and large doors for parachute drops. More than 10,000 Dakotas were built.

Soldiers called the C-47 a "Gooney Bird".

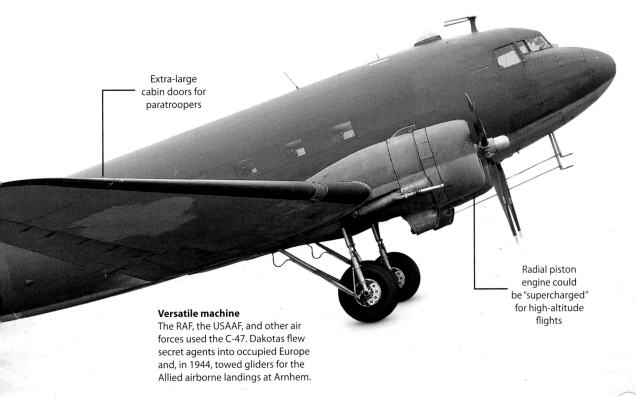

Extra-large cabin doors for paratroopers

Radial piston engine could be "supercharged" for high-altitude flights

Versatile machine
The RAF, the USAAF, and other air forces used the C-47. Dakotas flew secret agents into occupied Europe and, in 1944, towed gliders for the Allied airborne landings at Arnhem.

P-51 MUSTANG

The P-51 Mustang was the best US fighter of World War II, yet it almost failed. In 1940, Britain ordered Mustangs from the US. First tests did not impress, so a new engine was tried, the Merlin. It transformed the Mustang. The best model, the P-51D, could outfly most fighters.

SPECIFICATIONS

Size	11.3 m (37 ft) / 9.83 m (32 ft 3 in)	Speed	703 kph (437 mph)
Crew	1	Arms	Six 12.7 mm (0.5 in) machine guns; bombs and rockets

In a dive, a Mustang flew so fast the strain popped out rivets holding its metal plates together.

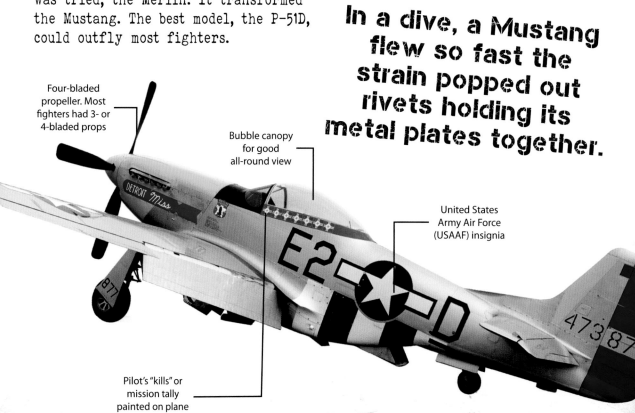

Four-bladed propeller. Most fighters had 3- or 4-bladed props

Bubble canopy for good all-round view

United States Army Air Force (USAAF) insignia

Pilot's "kills" or mission tally painted on plane

All rounder
The Mustang could do almost any job – escort bombers, attack ground targets such as trains and tanks, and win air battles against enemy fighters. More than 15,000 Mustangs were built.

BOMBER ESCORT

A Mustang could fly much further than other fighters – from England to Germany. One of its vital jobs was to escort Allied bombers into occupied Europe. Mustangs escorted the bombers, ready to take on German aircraft waiting to attack. Bomber pilots felt safer with the little Mustangs flying up above.

FOCKE-WULF FW-190

Most German fighter pilots thought the FW-190 better than the Me-109. It flew into battle in 1941, and at once alarmed Allied pilots. The new German fighter had guns in both nose and wings, and was big enough to carry bombs as well. Extra under-wing fuel tanks gave it an impressive flying range of up to 800 km (500 miles).

SPECIFICATIONS

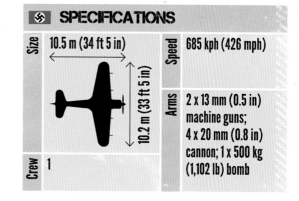

Size	10.5 m (34 ft 5 in) / 10.2 m (33 ft 5 in)	Speed	685 kph (426 mph)
Crew	1	Arms	2 x 13 mm (0.5 in) machine guns; 4 x 20 mm (0.8 in) cannon; 1 x 500 kg (1,102 lb) bomb

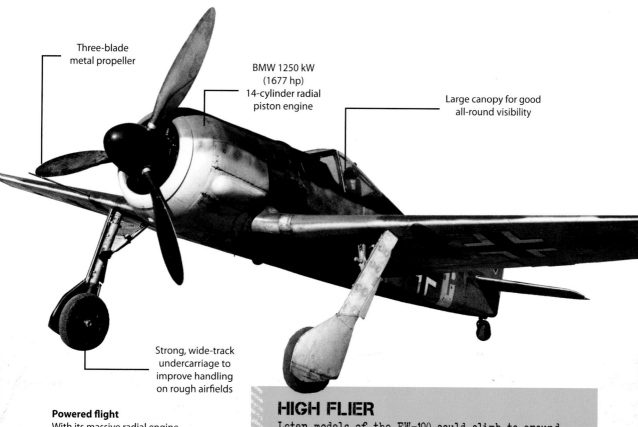

Three-blade metal propeller

BMW 1250 kW (1677 hp) 14-cylinder radial piston engine

Large canopy for good all-round visibility

Strong, wide-track undercarriage to improve handling on rough airfields

Powered flight
With its massive radial engine up front, the FW-190 looked a bit like its even bigger US rival, the P-47 Thunderbolt.

HIGH FLIER

Later models of the FW-190 could climb to around 12,000 m (39,000 ft), waiting to attack Allied bombers from above. High-flying 190s had a pressurized cockpit, bigger wings, and an engine-booster to maintain speed when flying at the top of its range.

B-17

The B-17, one of the US's most famous bomber planes, first flew in 1935 under the name of "Boeing Model 299". By 1945, it was celebrated as the B-17 Flying Fortress. More than 12,000 B-17s were built to fly high in the skies above Europe or the Pacific and drop their bombs.

SPECIFICATIONS

Size	23 m (75 ft 6 in) / 30 m (98 ft 5 in)	Speed	462 kph (287 mph)
		Arms	13 x 12.7 mm (0.5 in) machine guns; 8,000 kg (17,500 lb) of bombs
Crew	9 or 10		

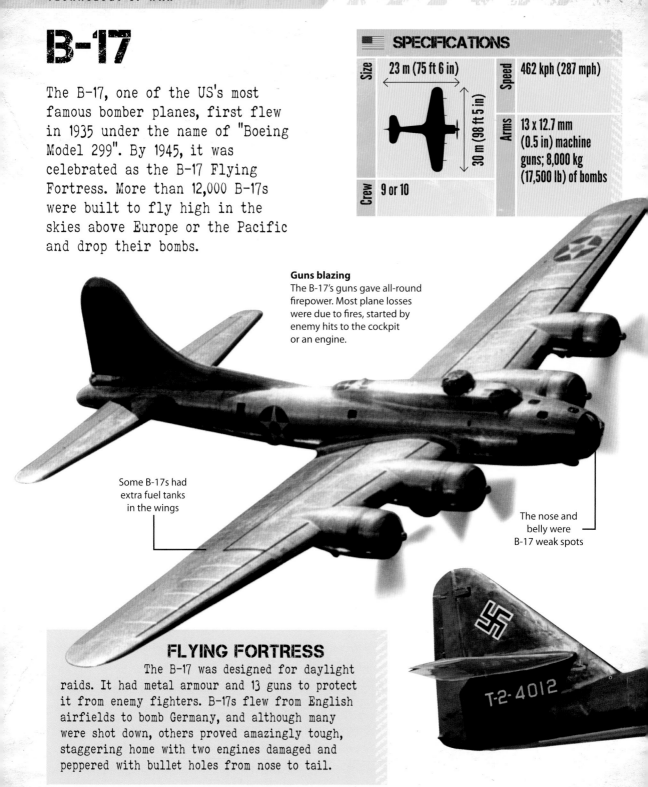

Guns blazing
The B-17's guns gave all-round firepower. Most plane losses were due to fires, started by enemy hits to the cockpit or an engine.

Some B-17s had extra fuel tanks in the wings

The nose and belly were B-17 weak spots

FLYING FORTRESS

The B-17 was designed for daylight raids. It had metal armour and 13 guns to protect it from enemy fighters. B-17s flew from English airfields to bomb Germany, and although many were shot down, others proved amazingly tough, staggering home with two engines damaged and peppered with bullet holes from nose to tail.

T-2-4012

ME-262

In 1944, the fastest propeller-driven fighter planes flew at about 690 kph (430 mph). So, when a German fighter roared in to attack at up to 870 kph (540 mph), Allied bomber crews gasped. This new aircraft had no propellers. It was the Messerschmitt Me-262 - the first jet plane to enter combat.

SPECIFICATIONS

Size		Speed	
10.6 m (34 ft 9 in) 12.5 m (40 ft 11 in)		870 kph (540 mph)	
Crew		Arms	
1		8 x 7.7mm (.303 in) machine guns in the wings	

SWALLOW

Named Schwalbe (meaning "Swallow"), the Me-262 was a twin-engine jet. Mistakenly, Hitler ordered the jets to carry bombs at first, which slowed them down. Without bombs, the Me-262 could fly faster than any Allied fighter. It attacked Allied bombers so fast, air-gunners hardly saw it coming.

Me-262s dived at high speed from above to dodge Allied bombers, then zoomed in behind to attack.

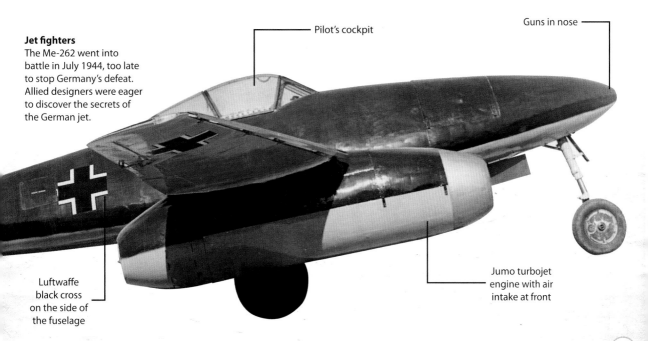

Jet fighters
The Me-262 went into battle in July 1944, too late to stop Germany's defeat. Allied designers were eager to discover the secrets of the German jet.

Pilot's cockpit

Guns in nose

Luftwaffe black cross on the side of the fuselage

Jumo turbojet engine with air intake at front

IL-2 STURMOVIK

The Russian Army used the Il-2 Sturmovik as a "flying tank". Sturmoviks flew over battlefields like angry wasps, shooting at enemy troops and tanks with guns, bombs, and rockets. Over 40,000 Il-2s were built in World War II, more than any other military aircraft.

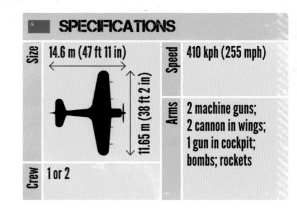

SPECIFICATIONS

Size	14.6 m (47 ft 11 in) / 11.65 m (38 ft 2 in)
Speed	410 kph (255 mph)
Arms	2 machine guns; 2 cannon in wings; 1 gun in cockpit; bombs; rockets
Crew	1 or 2

The cockpit was designed to hold two crew, but was later modified to hold just one

Hunchback
Germans nicknamed the Il-2 the "Hunchback", for its cockpit shape. In the 2-seat plane, the second crewman fired a rear-pointing gun.

The "flying tank" was heavily armoured against ground gunfire

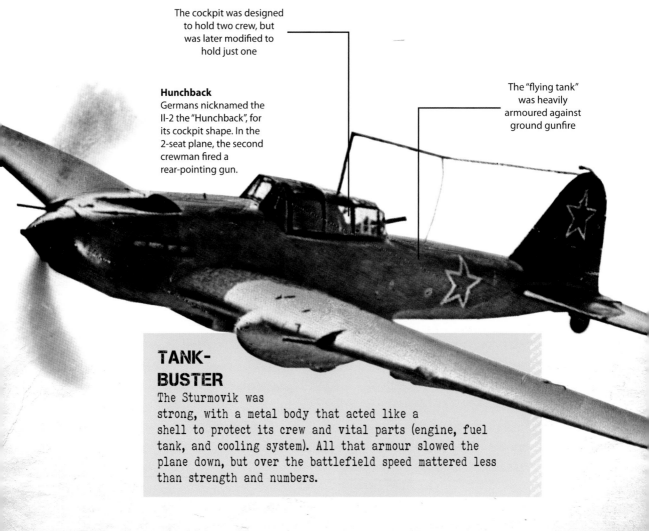

TANK-BUSTER

The Sturmovik was strong, with a metal body that acted like a shell to protect its crew and vital parts (engine, fuel tank, and cooling system). All that armour slowed the plane down, but over the battlefield speed mattered less than strength and numbers.

MXY-7 OHKA

The MXY-7 Ohka ("Cherry Blossom") was a Japanese suicide plane, made to attack Allied shipping in the Pacific – and simple enough for an untrained pilot to fly. A bigger plane carried the Okha up, and let it go when a target was sighted. The pilot glided at first, then fired the rocket engines, and aimed for the target.

SPECIFICATIONS

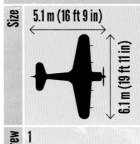

Size	5.1 m (16 ft 9 in) 6.1 m (19 ft 11 in)	Speed	643 kph (400 mph) or higher in a dive
		Arms	Explosive warhead in the nose
Crew	1		

The Ohka was built to fly only once.

Cheaply built bodywork

No-return rocket
The Ohka had three rocket motors for speed. The Japanese also tried a jet engine. The idea – to make a cheap, quick "bomber-killer" – did not work.

Warhead weighing 1,100 kg (2,500 lb) in nose

FLYING BOMB

The Ohka had a warhead in its nose to blow a ship apart, but few Ohkas got close to their targets. The slow aircraft carrying the rocket-plane was easily shot down, and most suicide pilots were killed before starting their attack.

Seat for suicide pilot in cabin

WATERCRAFT

Ships, submarines, and other craft saw action in all kinds of waters, from the frozen Arctic and cold, grey North Atlantic to the vast Pacific Ocean. The war at sea involved some of the war's biggest machines: battleships and aircraft carriers. Many small craft also took part, including some that could emerge from the water to fight on dry land.

DUKW

The DUKW, or "duck" as many Allied soldiers called it, was an amphibious truck. This utility, all-wheel drive vehicle, designed in 1942, was one of the war's engineering success stories. It was built in the US by General Motors, who put a boat hull and propeller on a six-wheeled army truck.

SPECIFICATIONS

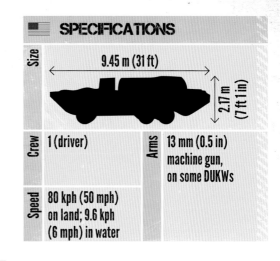

Size	9.45 m (31 ft)		2.17 m (7 ft 1 in)
Crew	1 (driver)	**Arms**	13 mm (0.5 in) machine gun, on some DUKWs
Speed	80 kph (50 mph) on land; 9.6 kph (6 mph) in water		

HOW THE DUKW WORKED

On land, the DUKW drove like a truck. In water, it floated and the engine drove the propeller to push it along. The DUKW had little armour to protect it, but it could move troops and supplies from ship to shore, or across rivers and lakes.

Canvas soft-top for bad weather

Headlight and fenders to protect the hull

Boat-shaped hull for water

Swimming duck
Experts found it hard to believe that the DUKW would "swim". Seeing it rescue coast guards from a stormy sea changed their minds. DUKWs even crossed the English Channel.

JAPANESE NAVY ZUIKAKU

The Japanese hoped aircraft carriers such as Zuikaku would defeat the US Navy in the Pacific. Zuikaku took part in the attack on Pearl Harbor in December 1941. It then fought through the battles of the Coral Sea (1942) and Philippine Sea (1944).

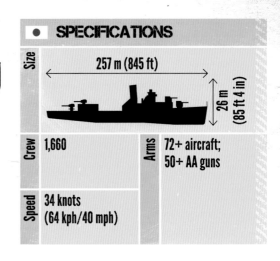

● SPECIFICATIONS

Size	257 m (845 ft)	26 m (85 ft 4 in)
Crew	1,660	Arms: 72+ aircraft; 50+ AA guns
Speed	34 knots (64 kph/40 mph)	

LAST TO GO

By late 1944, Zuikaku was the last of the six Pearl Harbor aircraft carriers still afloat. Its war ended on 25 October, when Allied planes sank it off Cape Engano in the Philippines. Hit by US bombs and torpedoes, Zuikaku went down with more than 800 sailors, including the captain.

Maiden voyage
Zuikaku (which means "lucky crane") was launched in September 1941. In November she left for Pearl Harbor carrying 84 planes.

USS YORKTOWN

USS Yorktown, with sister ships Enterprise and Hornet, were not the biggest US Navy aircraft carriers, yet they became as famous as any Allied warship. Yorktown and Hornet were both sunk in battles against the Japanese. Only Enterprise outlasted the war, having fought in almost every Pacific naval battle.

SPECIFICATIONS

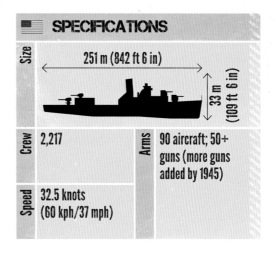

Size	251 m (842 ft 6 in)	33 m (109 ft 6 in)
Crew	2,217	
Arms	90 aircraft; 50+ guns (more guns added by 1945)	
Speed	32.5 knots (60 kph/37 mph)	

JAPANESE ATTACK

USS Yorktown was hit by Japanese dive-bombers and lost at the Battle of Midway. USS Hornet was sunk by torpedo in 1943. In all, USS Enterprise sank 71 enemy ships and damaged almost 200. In 1945 a kamikaze blasted a hole in the flight deck.

Preparing for combat
In 1942, USS Yorktown was taken into dry dock at Pearl Harbor, Hawaii, and prepared for the Battle of Midway.

The decks swarm with people as the carrier is readied for battle

GATO SUBMARINE

USS Gato gave its name to a class (group) of US Navy submarines. Most US subs had fish names. A gato is a small shark, but Gato was a big submarine. Its crew enjoyed more comforts than other submariners, with refrigerators, washing machines, and a bunk for each man.

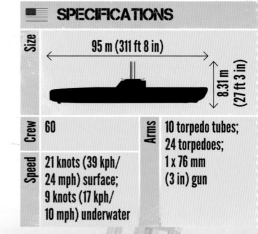

🇺🇸 SPECIFICATIONS

Size	95 m (311 ft 8 in) — 8.31 m (27 ft 3 in)
Crew	60
Speed	21 knots (39 kph/ 24 mph) surface; 9 knots (17 kph/ 10 mph) underwater
Arms	10 torpedo tubes; 24 torpedoes; 1 x 76 mm (3 in) gun

Going down
A Gato submarine could dive 90 m (300 ft) deep to miss depth charges dropped from enemy ships. It had 10 torpedo tubes to hit back.

Deck gun to fire at ships on the surface

GATOS AT WAR
Prowling the Pacific, Gato-class submarines sank two big Japanese carriers and many other smaller ships. Their main weapons were underwater torpedoes and a big deck gun to deal with cargo ships. But US torpedoes could be a problem at times, turning in circles back towards their own submarine!

TYPE XXI

The German Type XXI (21) submarine "Electroboat" outsmarted all rivals. It was big, fast, and could dive 250 m (820 ft). It hunted using sonar (sound-echo), fired torpedoes at high speed, and cruised for 21,000 km (13,000 miles). Most WWII submarines just dived for a short time. Type XXI stayed under.

SPECIFICATIONS

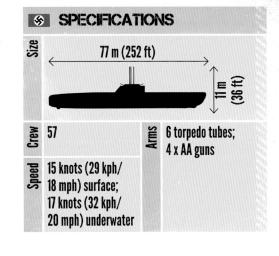

Size	77 m (252 ft) / 11 m (36 ft)
Crew	57
Arms	6 torpedo tubes; 4 x AA guns
Speed	15 knots (29 kph/18 mph) surface; 17 knots (32 kph/20 mph) underwater

Snorkel sucked in air to charge batteries under water

Radar antenna on snorkel mast

Conning tower with periscope and snorkel tube

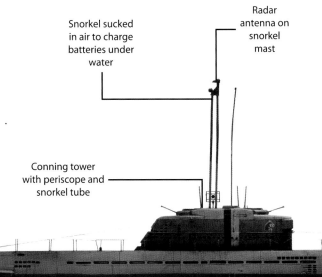

The Type XXI was the first submarine designed to operate fully submerged.

Super-sub
The Type XXI's hull was shaped like the number 8. The crew, engines, and weapons were on top, with fuel tanks underneath. Unusually, it was faster under water than on the surface.

Streamlined hull for extra speed under water

A TRUE SUBMARINE

Type XXI could stay underwater for two days, using electricity from battery cells. On the surface it used diesel engines, like all WWII submarines. The Germans tried hard to build more super-subs, but had only four when the war ended. The Allies were eager to know their secrets.

HMS BELFAST

Cruisers were warships that were smaller than battleships and carriers. Their main weapons were medium-sized guns and torpedoes. HMS Belfast was a British navy cruiser. Damaged by a magnetic mine in 1939, it returned in autumn 1942 to fight at the battle of North Cape, helping to sink the German battlecruiser Scharnhorst.

🇬🇧 SPECIFICATIONS

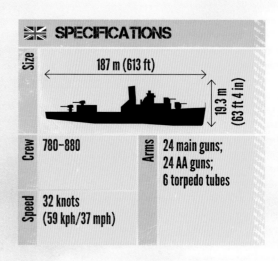

Size	187 m (613 ft) × 19.3 m (63 ft 4 in)
Crew	780–880
Arms	24 main guns; 24 AA guns; 6 torpedo tubes
Speed	32 knots (59 kph/37 mph)

ARCTIC CONVOYS AND D-DAY

HMS Belfast escorted Allied convoys through the Arctic to the Soviet Union, fighting off German air attacks. In June 1944, she was off the beaches of Normandy, guns firing at German defences. HMS Belfast outlived the war and later saw action in Korea. She is now a museum ship in London.

HMS Belfast had a fully equipped sick bay and three surgeons on board to treat casualties.

Turret with 15 cm (6 in) guns

Hull protected by metal "belt" armour

USS FLETCHER

USS Fletcher DD-445 gave its name to the best class (group) of US destroyers. There were 175 Fletchers that went to war from 1941 to 1945. Every wartime navy had destroyers – medium to small warships that were heavily armed against submarines or warships often bigger than themselves.

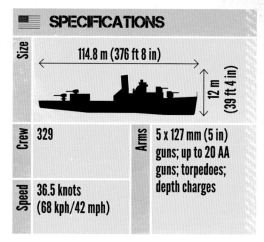

SPECIFICATIONS

Size 114.8 m (376 ft 8 in) | 12 m (39 ft 4 in)

Crew 329

Speed 36.5 knots (68 kph/42 mph)

Arms 5 x 127 mm (5 in) guns; up to 20 AA guns; torpedoes; depth charges

WEAPONRY ON THE WAVES

Warships were fairly easy targets from the air, so destroyers had plenty of anti-aircraft (AA) guns. The Fletchers had 40 mm (1.5 in) Bofors AA guns and smaller quick-firing Oerlikon cannons. They could fire torpedoes, lay smoke screens, and drop depth charges on lurking submarines.

Full steam ahead!
Destroyers such as USS Fletcher could out-speed most warships. They needed good AA guns to fight off enemy air attacks.

USS MISSOURI

Missouri was one of four "Iowa-class" battleships – the US Navy's biggest. At 52,600 tonnes, Missouri was also bigger than Germany's Bismarck, and longer than the giant Japanese battleships Yamato and Musashi. Missouri fought in the Pacific, where it was damaged by a Japanese kamikaze (suicide plane).

🇺🇸 SPECIFICATIONS

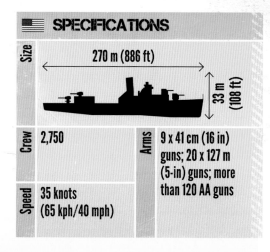

Size	270 m (886 ft) — 33 m (108 ft)
Crew	2,750
Speed	35 knots (65 kph/40 mph)
Arms	9 x 41 cm (16 in) guns; 20 x 127 m (5-in) guns; more than 120 AA guns

BATTLESHIP FINALE

Big battleships were no longer battle-winners at sea. Their size made them easy targets for WWII aircraft and submarines. But their big guns could destroy targets miles inland, and in this way helped Allied landings in Europe and the Pacific.

Radar antenna

Surrender on deck
Missouri won its place in history in September 1945. The Japanese signed their surrender on the battleship's deck, to end World War II. It is now a museum ship at Pearl Harbor, Hawaii.

Conning tower for command and gun control

41 cm (16 in) guns in triple turrets

TORPEDO BOAT

A US Navy Patrol Torpedo ("PT") boat was a fast motor boat, smaller than most warships, but well armed. PT boats could defend ports, speed up rivers, and patrol coasts. These craft were very fast and possessed guns, torpedoes, and used depth charges as weapons.

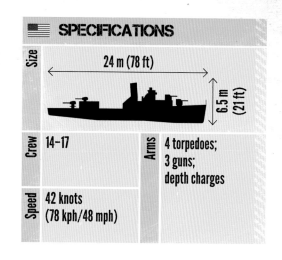

SPECIFICATIONS

Size	24 m (78 ft) — 6.5 m (21 ft)
Crew	14–17
Arms	4 torpedoes; 3 guns; depth charges
Speed	42 knots (78 kph/48 mph)

POWER BOATS

The US Navy had two kinds of PT boat, the Elco and the Higgins, both about the same size. To ride buffeting waves at speed, the boats had to be strong. Their big engines powered them along as fast as a car.

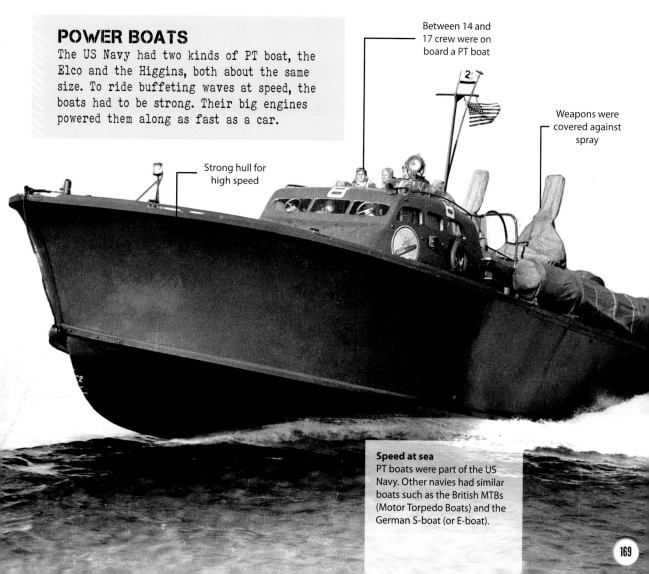

Between 14 and 17 crew were on board a PT boat

Weapons were covered against spray

Strong hull for high speed

Speed at sea
PT boats were part of the US Navy. Other navies had similar boats such as the British MTBs (Motor Torpedo Boats) and the German S-boat (or E-boat).

ARTILLERY

Artillery refers to any gun or rocket weapon too big to be
carried by one person. In World War II, armies had heavy guns
that needed tractors to pull them, self-propelled guns mounted
on motorized vehicles, and light guns that could be packed on
a mule's back or on a jeep.

MORTAR

Soldiers liked the mortar because it was simple. It fired a small bomb-like missile high into the air to land on the enemy. The mortar was small enough to carry, and was easy to hide. For these same reasons, soldiers hated mortars being used against them.

SPECIFICATIONS

Size	1.4 m (4 ft 6 in) barrel; weight: 51 kg (112 lb)
Crew	3
Range	2,286 m (7,500 ft)
Missile	High explosive, smoke, or star shells (to light up the night sky)

HOW IT WORKED

The mortar was a metal tube on a stand. It had a base plate to take the shock of recoil as it fired. At the lower end of the tube was a firing pin. The gunner dropped a small mortar bomb into the muzzle end. The bomb hit the pin, and fired up into the air.

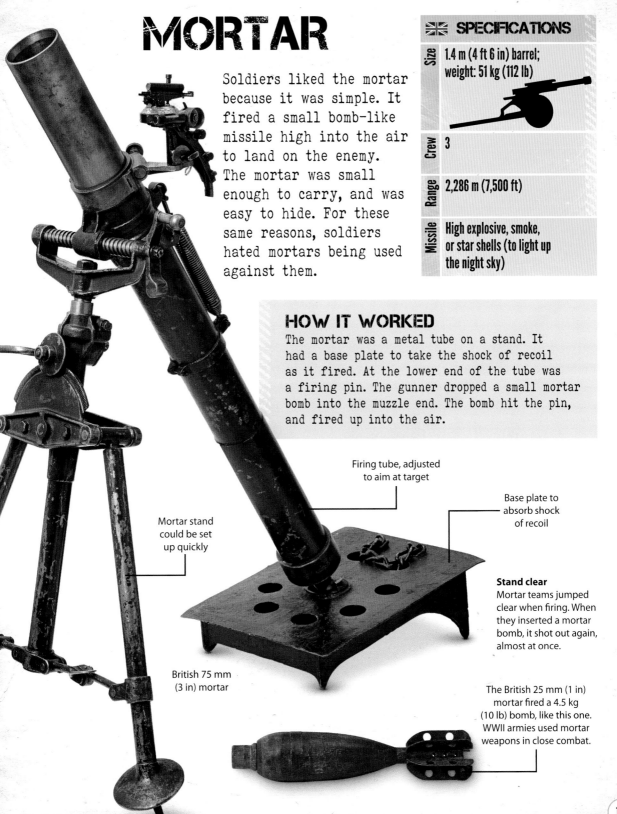

Firing tube, adjusted to aim at target

Base plate to absorb shock of recoil

Mortar stand could be set up quickly

Stand clear
Mortar teams jumped clear when firing. When they inserted a mortar bomb, it shot out again, almost at once.

British 75 mm (3 in) mortar

The British 25 mm (1 in) mortar fired a 4.5 kg (10 lb) bomb, like this one. WWII armies used mortar weapons in close combat.

GERMAN AA GUN

Anti-aircraft guns, or Flak guns, were put in place to save troops, ships, or cities from aircraft attack. There were two main types of AA gun. Heavy guns fired at high-flying planes. Smaller, quick-firing guns shot at low-level attack aircraft.

SPECIFICATIONS

Size	Barrel: 5 m (16 ft); gun: 5.8 m (20 ft) x 2.1 m (6 ft 11 in); weight: 7,500 kg (16,000 lb)
Crew	6 (could vary)
Range	11,000 m (36,000 ft)
Missile	88 mm shell weighing 9 kg (20 lb)

Long barrel for high-velocity shell

The 88 mm
German gunners operate a Flak 36 anti-aircraft gun with a calibre of 88 mm.

FIND AND DESTROY

AA gun crews spotted enemy aircraft using radar or their own eyesight. They worked out its speed and course, aimed their guns, and fired shells up to 10,600 m (35,000 ft) in the air. A "proximity fuze" exploded the shell when it was close enough to destroy the plane.

The 88 mm Flak 36 was also used as an anti-tank gun.

Recuperator helps barrel to return to its firing position

Legs keep the gun stable

SELF-PROPELLED US M7 GUN

Big artillery guns are cumbersome, so are transported on vehicles with wheels or tank tracks. This makes them self-propelled, so they can go almost anywhere on the battlefield. The US M7 was used on D-Day (1944) and at the Battle of the Bulge (1944-45).

SPECIFICATIONS

Size	6 m (19 ft) x 2.95 m (9 ft 8 in); weight: 23,000 kg (50,640 lb)
Crew	5
Range	11,000 m (36,000 ft)
Missile	105 mm (4 in) howitzer; 1.3 cm (0.5 in) machine gun

PACKING A PUNCH

The M7 had a 105 mm (4 in) howitzer - a gun that fired shells high in the air to hit targets hidden by trees or houses. The M7 was as useful in town battles in Europe as in the jungles of Burma. Soldiers thought its front looked like a church pulpit, so they called it the "Priest".

In action
An M7 "Priest" and its crew of operators in the field.

Heavy machine gun

Main 105 mm (4 in) howitzer

The M7 was built on the body of an M3 Lee or M4 Sherman tank.

FINALIST

KATYUSHA ROCKET

Russian Katyusha rockets terrified the enemy, as they fell in hundreds from the sky. They were frightening to fire, too, whooshing from the back of trucks. Some trucks had up to 48 launch-racks, and they could also be fitted to tanks, trains, and boats.

SPECIFICATIONS

Size	Rocket: 1.8 m (5 ft 11 in) long
Crew	4
Range	8,000 m (26,250 ft)
Missile	High explosive rocket warhead: weight 5 kg (11 lb)

QUICK FIRE

The Russians fired their rockets in great numbers. They were easy to make, easy to fire, and could destroy enemy defences before a ground attack. Katyusha rocket attacks were quick. Crews could fire all their rockets in under 10 seconds.

Germans called the rockets "Stalin's Organ" after their howling noise.

Launch rails on steel racks fixed to trucks

BM-13 launch truck

Load and fire
It could take up to an hour to reload the rocket racks after firing. To aim, the crew angled the racks at 45 degrees, then fired.

NEBELWERFER

The German Army also used battlefield rocket launchers. The Nebelwerfer, or "smoke-thrower", had barrels that fired rockets with high-explosive warheads. The Nebelwerfer was used as an artillery weapon on the ground, but it was also used to shoot down Allied bombers.

SPECIFICATIONS

Size
1.3 m (4 ft 4 in) barrel; weight 550 kg (1,200 lb)

Crew
4

Range
7,850 m (25,755 ft)

Missile
112 kg (248 lb) rockets

Rocket barrels

The Allies called it "Moaning Minnie" because of the eerie sound it made.

Carriage on wheels for transportation

SMOKE AND GAS

Before WWII, many people feared poison gas might be used as a weapon, as it had been in WWI. The Nebelwerfer could have fired gas weapons, but never did. Armies in WWII did use smoke shells, but not chemical weapons such as poison gas.

Kickback
The Nebelwerfer fired its rockets one after another, before being reloaded. The crew took shelter from a "kickback" of dust and stones from the rocket's exhaust.

Trails that rested on the ground

SECRET WEAPONS

Scientists and engineers went to war in laboratories and secret test bases, working on ideas for new and terrifying weapons to help them win the war. Among many interesting, but useless, ideas were "robot boats", "ray guns", and "sound-cannons". Most brilliant ideas stayed on the drawing board, but some were actually built, and a few of them - radar, sonar, rockets, and the atom bomb - changed the war.

BOMBING BEAMS

In June 1940, Britain learned of a new German bombing aid. Called Knickebein (German for "crooked leg"), it guided bombers to targets by day or night, even in thick cloud. Pilots followed radio beams and, where two beams crossed over a target, a timer in the plane set the bombs to drop.

SPECIFICATIONS

Size/Range	Original antenna 30 m (100 ft) high. Beam was 1,600 km (1 mile) wide
Operator	German air force
Date	1940
Inventor	Johannes Plendl (Germany)

BOMBER CLUE

The British found a clue to the beam system in a shot-down Heinkel III bomber. Its radio operator's log book noted "Radio Beam Knickebein". Later, the British worked out how to jam this system. However, the Germans then fitted different types, and continued to use radio beams successfully.

Crew's "X-box" receiver to pick up radio beams

Clockwork bomb timer released bombs

German Heinkel III bomber

Lower machine gun position

Coventry Blitz
On 14 November 1940, the Knickebein system guided 450 Heinkel III bombers from the elite Luftwaffe KGr100 squadron to attack Coventry in England.

The Knickebein beam was named after a magic crow from a folk tale that could see in the dark.

RADAR

In 1940, Britain had 30 new secret radar stations on its coast, from Cornwall in the far west, to Newcastle in the northeast. Radar gave early warning of incoming bombers, so fighter planes could get airborne, ready to attack them.

SPECIFICATIONS

Size/Range	3/4 steel masts x 110 m (360ft) high
Operator	British air force
Date	1935–1940
Inventor	Robert Watson-Watt and others

THE BIRTH OF RADAR

Pioneers in the early 1900s found radio waves "bounced off" objects. In 1904, German engineer Christian Hulsmeyer invented ship radar, to prevent ships colliding at sea. In 1935, British scientist Robert Watson Watt invented air radar, which could pick up echoes bounced from planes 320 km (200 miles) away.

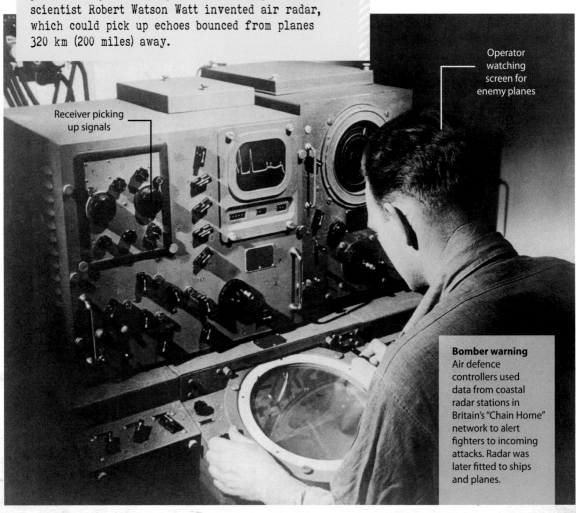

Operator watching screen for enemy planes

Receiver picking up signals

Bomber warning
Air defence controllers used data from coastal radar stations in Britain's "Chain Home" network to alert fighters to incoming attacks. Radar was later fitted to ships and planes.

SONAR

Sonar used sound echoes to hunt for submarines. A ship sent out sound waves and listened for "pings" or echoes from any submarine the sound waves hit. The system was developed as "asdic" in Britain and later as "sonar" in the US. Asdic was short for "Anti-Submarine Detection and Investigation Committee".

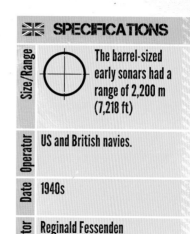

SPECIFICATIONS

Size/Range	The barrel-sized early sonars had a range of 2,200 m (7,218 ft)
Operator	US and British navies.
Date	1940s
Inventor	Reginald Fessenden (Canada) 1912

Headphones for listening to instructions

SONAR

In the US, the name sonar was used from 1942. It was short for **S**ound **N**avigation **A**nd **R**adar, and was fitted to destroyers and other submarine-hunting ships. From the echoes, a sonar operator could tell how far away a submarine was and what course it was steering.

Setting charge to correct depth

Depth-charge operator
Once the position and depth of an enemy submarine had been identified by sonar, an operator set the charge to explode close to the sub.

CODE-BREAKERS

Code-breakers were often good at maths, crosswords, or puzzles. At an English country house called Bletchley Park, a team worked to try to break the German codes. Few outside knew what went on at Bletchley Park, or "Station X", and all who worked there were sworn to secrecy.

 SPECIFICATIONS

Size/Range	Colossus filled one side of a room
Operator	British intelligence
Date	1943 and 1944, Britain
Inventor	Tommy Flowers and others (Britain)

COLOSSUS

Groups of code-breakers worked in small huts. There were chess players, language experts, people from universities, and engineers who knew about electronics and communications. The engineers built a code-breaking machine, the world's first electronic computer, and named it Colossus.

Grand calculator
Colossus could crack Nazi codes, but was not really an "all-purpose" computer like the type we have today. It functioned more like a giant calculator.

Operator with Colossus Mark 2

ENIGMA MACHINE

Each side in WWII sent out a daily stream of messages, with battle plans, orders, and information from secret agents. To keep them secret, messages were sent in code. The Germans had a machine – Enigma – to make up codes. They thought it was unbeatable, but they were wrong.

SPECIFICATIONS

Size/Range	34 cm (13.5 in) x 15 cm (6 in) box
Operator	German military
Date	1919 to 1940s
Inventor	Arthur Scherbius, 1918 (Germany)

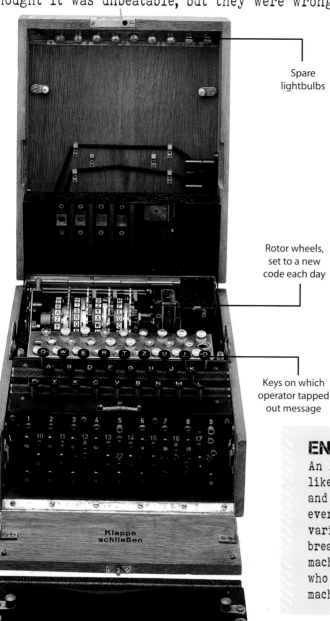

Spare lightbulbs

Rotor wheels, set to a new code each day

Keys on which operator tapped out message

Klappe schließen

Well-kept secret
From 1940, the Allies could read almost all German secret signals. They called this priceless information "Ultra" and made sure it was top secret. The Germans never knew their messages were being read.

Messages had to be kept short. Long messages were split up and sent in different codes.

ENIGMA VARIATIONS

An Enigma code-making machine looked like a typewriter, with toothed wheels and keys. It could change the code used every day, with millions of different variations. In 1939, Polish code-breakers got hold of some Enigma machines and gave them to the Allies, who cracked the secrets of the Enigma machine within six months.

BOUNCING BOMBS

In 1943, the RAF attacked three dams in Germany. There were 19 Lancasters in the raid and each had to drop a unique "bouncing bomb". The planes had to fly at exactly 355 kph (220 mph), 20 m (65 ft) above the water, and drop the bomb 150 m (490 ft) from the target. The "bouncing bomb" then skipped over the water, like a stone skimming across a pond, to hit the dam.

SPECIFICATIONS

Size/Range	152 cm (60 in) x 127 cm (50 in)
Operator	British air force
Date	1943
Inventor	Barnes Wallis

TESTING THE BOMB

The bomb's inventor was Barnes Wallis, who also designed the RAF's Wellington bomber. To help judge the right height from which to drop the bomb, aircrews tried shining two lights onto the water. When the beams met, it meant the plane was at the right height.

The bomb was slung beneath the Lancaster. It was made to spin, to help it bounce.

Bomber crews were hand-picked

Expert fliers
The Dambuster squadron (No. 617) was selected from fliers with expert skills as pilots, navigators, or bomb aimers. They practised hard to perfect the new secret weapon.

RADIO-GUIDED BOMB

Most bombs in WWII were simply dropped from a bomber. The Hs-293 was one of the first guided missiles, steered onto its target by radio. This radio-guided bomb came as a surprise to the Allies when the Germans first used it in 1943 to attack shipping.

	SPECIFICATIONS	
Size/Range		3.8 m (12.5 ft) long x 3 m (10 ft) wide
Operator	German air force	
Date	1942 from 1939 design	
Inventor	Herbert Wagner and Henschel company, Germany	

GLIDE-BOMB

The Hs-293 was carried under a bomber, such as the Dorner 217 or Heinkel 177. A big missile, it was more than 3.8 m (12 ft 6 in) long, and could carry a 295 kg (650 lb) warhead. The aircraft took it to 4,000 m (12,000 ft) before the drop, so it could build up speed as it glided down to the target.

On target
The Hs-293 first sank a British ship and later a US troopship off Algeria. The Allies tried to beat it by "jamming" the radio-control system.

The Germans also planned a radio-controlled "diving missile" to travel under water.

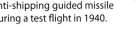

A Heinkel He-111 drops a Hs-293 anti-shipping guided missile during a test flight in 1940.

V-1 FLYING BOMB

In 1944, Adolf Hitler promised that new "Vengeance weapons" would turn likely defeat into victory. Invented in secret by German scientists, they would shock the world. The first "V-weapon" was the V-1. It was a flying bomb, with a jet engine, but no pilot. The first V-1 hit London on 13 June 1944.

SPECIFICATIONS

Size/Range	8.3 m (27 ft) long x 1.4 m (4 ft 6 in) high
Operator	German air force
Date	1944
Inventor	Robert Lusser and Fieseler Co.

A fighter could "flip" over a V-1 in the air by tipping its wing, so it crashed before it could do any harm.

Warhead in the nose

Pulse-jet engine giving a speed of 650 kph (404 mph)

Wide range
The V-1 had a maximum range of 200 km (125 miles). Initially, its raids on Britain were very succesful.

DOODLE-BUG

The V-1 was launched from a ramp. Its simple guidance-control cut the engine over the target, so the bomb crashed and exploded. A fast fighter could shoot down a V-1, making it crash harmlessly into the sea. The V-1's droning engine gave it the nickname "doodle-bug" (an insect).

The V-1 had stubby wings

ARADO 234

Germany never had a big bomber to match the B-17 or Lancaster, but it did make the world's first jet bomber. In 1944, the Arado 234 Blitz roared into combat. It was so quick that no Allied fighter could catch it.

SPECIFICATIONS

Size/Range	12.6 m (41 ft 6 in) long, span 14.4 ft (47 ft 3 in)
Operator	German air force
Date	1943
Inventor	Walter Blume and Arado Co.

BLITZ BLAST

With a speed of more than 720 kph (450 mph), the Arado 234 Blitz left all Allied fighters far behind, except the Meteor jet. With hundreds more Blitz bombers, instead of just 40, the war may have ended differently for Germany. But by 1944, the war was almost over in Europe. The thundering Blitz flew in too late.

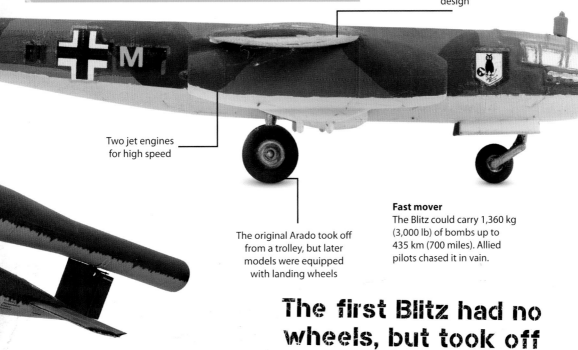

Unusual high-wing design

Two jet engines for high speed

The original Arado took off from a trolley, but later models were equipped with landing wheels

Fast mover
The Blitz could carry 1,360 kg (3,000 lb) of bombs up to 435 km (700 miles). Allied pilots chased it in vain.

The first Blitz had no wheels, but took off from a skateboard-like "trolley". Proper wheels were added later.

V-2

In October 1942, a large rocket took off in smoke and flames from Germany's secret rocket base at Peenemunde. It was the first V-2 to be launched, and flew 160 km (100 miles). The Allies knew of the new Nazi "super weapon", but were still shocked by the V-2 attacks that followed. Luckily, Allied troops soon overran the V-2 bases and factories.

SPECIFICATIONS

Size/Range	14 m (46 ft) high x 1.6 m (5 ft) wide
Operator	German army
Date	1942 (first test)
Inventor	Wernher von Braun and team (Germany)

The V-2 was supersonic, at 5,794 kph (3,600 mph), so nobody on the ground heard it coming.

Warhead in rocket nose

Fuel tanks were positioned in the middle of the rocket

Engines and steering close to tail

The missile age dawns
The V-2 was 14 m (46 ft) high and weighed over 12 tonnes (most of the weight being fuel). It flew too fast to be shot down.

Fins to keep the rocket steady in flight

READY FOR SPACE

The V-2 was the world's first big rocket that burned liquid-chemical fuel, and could reach the edge of space. After the war, the Soviet Union and America used V-2 secrets to build rockets that took astronauts to the Moon and beyond.

BACHEM NATTER

As the war in the air turned against the Nazis, their engineers came up with even more weird machines. In 1944, they rushed the Ba-349 Natter into production. Designed to attack high-flying Allied bombers, the Germans hoped that it would turn the war in their favour.

SPECIFICATIONS

Size/Range	6 m (19 ft 6 in) x 4 m (13 ft)
Operator	SS and German air force
Date	1945
Inventor	Erich Bachem, Germany

DESPERATE STAKES

The Natter was a desperate design. It was really a missile, launched like a rocket. The idea was for the pilot inside to fly straight up, heading for B-17s high above. When he spotted his target, the pilot would take the controls and fire rockets. Then he would glide away and bale out by parachute.

The Natter made just one test flight - it crashed, killing the pilot.

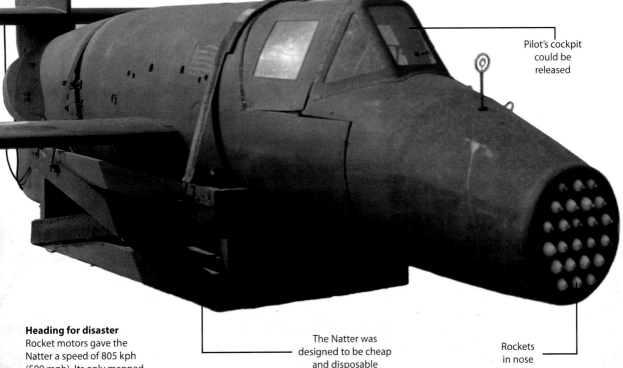

Pilot's cockpit could be released

Heading for disaster
Rocket motors gave the Natter a speed of 805 kph (500 mph). Its only manned flight ended in disaster.

The Natter was designed to be cheap and disposable

Rockets in nose

ROCKET PLANE

The Me-163 Komet was based on a 1930s German research glider. It was an unusual swept-wing shape, without a normal tail, and had a rocket motor. Tested in secret in 1941, it alarmed test pilots by its amazing speed. At 885 kph (550 mph) it was the world's fastest aircraft.

SPECIFICATIONS

Size/Range	9.3 m (30 ft 6 in) x 5.98 m (19ft 6 in)
Operator	German air force
Date	1941
Inventor	Alexander Lippisch and Messerschmitt Co.

Out of fuel
The Me-163's rocket soon burned out. The pilot hoped to glide down to a safe landing.

Rocket motor to boost climb at high speed.

191461

Landing skid

Swept-back wings

Wheels used for takeoff were discarded in the air

KOMETS IN COMBAT

The Me 163 went into action in May 1944, against Allied B-17 bombers over Germany. One problem was its speed. The plane flew so fast that the pilot had just three seconds to shoot his two guns before the Komet had rocketed past its target.

The Japanese copied the Me 163, building the J8M Shusui. Only one flew, but it crashed.

ATOM BOMB

The atom bombs dropped on the Japanese cities of Hiroshima and Nagasaki, in August 1945, ended World War II. The race to build an atom bomb had begun in the 1930s, with "nuclear fission" experiments in Germany. However, some scientists fled the Nazis to join the Allies, and helped Britain and the USA to develop the bomb in what was known as the Manhattan Project.

SPECIFICATIONS

Size/Range	"Little Boy" – 3 m (10 ft) long, weight 4,400 kg (9,700 lb)
Operator	US Army Air Force
Date	1945
Inventor	Francis Birch (USA) and Manhattan Project team

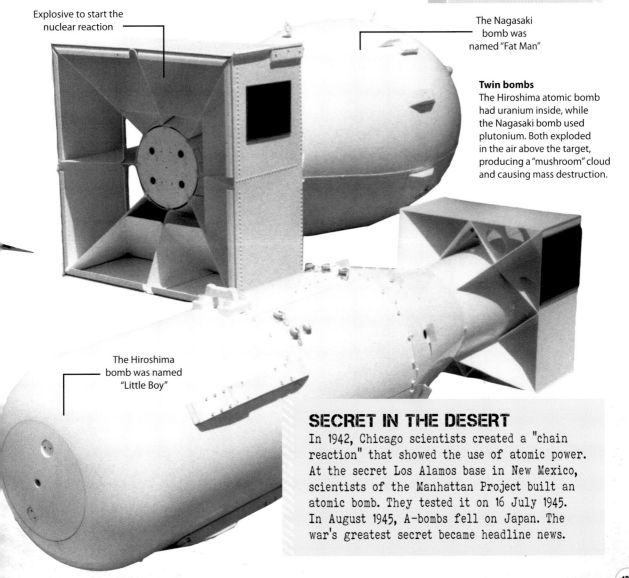

Explosive to start the nuclear reaction

The Nagasaki bomb was named "Fat Man"

Twin bombs
The Hiroshima atomic bomb had uranium inside, while the Nagasaki bomb used plutonium. Both exploded in the air above the target, producing a "mushroom" cloud and causing mass destruction.

The Hiroshima bomb was named "Little Boy"

SECRET IN THE DESERT

In 1942, Chicago scientists created a "chain reaction" that showed the use of atomic power. At the secret Los Alamos base in New Mexico, scientists of the Manhattan Project built an atomic bomb. They tested it on 16 July 1945. In August 1945, A-bombs fell on Japan. The war's greatest secret became headline news.

REFERENCE SECTION

World War II was the most destructive war in
history. For six years, war raged across Europe,
Africa, Asia, and the Pacific. When it ended in
1945, world borders were redrawn and nations were
left to count the terrible cost – in both economic
damage and human lives. As many as 55 million
people were killed in the conflict, including
10 million Jews, Gypsies, and other minorities
murdered by the Nazis in the Holocaust.

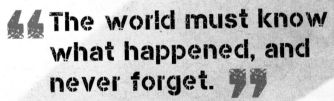

**"The world must know
what happened, and
never forget. "**

US General Eisenhower
visiting Holocaust death camps in 1945

IN THIS CHAPTER:

WHY THE WORLD WENT TO WAR

World War II started in 1939, but the seeds of war were sown after World War I (1914-1918). In Germany, Adolf Hitler, leader of the Nazi party, built up a powerful armed force, and formed an alliance, known as the Axis, with Italy and Japan. All three nations had similar aims - to gain more power and territory.

THE RISE OF FASCISM

Mussolini came to power in Italy in the 1920s. Hitler came to power in Germany in the 1930s. Both leaders believed in Fascism - a political system in which the government and the armed forces had supreme power, and opponents were jailed or killed. Stalin followed similar policies in the USSR in the name of Communism. The Nazis in Germany outlawed all opposition, persecuted Jews, and wanted a new German Empire. Japan also had a military government, and dreamed of a new empire in Asia.

THE ARMS RACE

As the Axis grew stronger, France, Britain, and the US slowly realised they must make new weapons ("re-arm"). By the late 1930s, all the leading nations had started to build up their armies, navies, and air forces. Japan went to war in China, and Italy attacked Abyssinia (Ethiopia). Confident he would not be stopped, Hitler demanded more territory, taking over Austria. The Nazis became more threatening, forcing many Jewish families to become refugees. Still Britain and France did not want war, and in the US, most people wanted no part in any new European conflict.

Huge Nazi parades were held across Germany, and propaganda was used to twist the truth, and rally the German people behind their "Führer" (leader).

KEEPING THE PEACE

In 1938, the memory of the horror of World War I was still strong. Britain and France did not want a second world war. Their governments tried to keep the peace (or at least delay war) by "appeasing" Hitler and giving him the territory he wanted. The League of Nations (an international organisation) was supposed to stop wars, but it had not prevented Japan attacking China or Italy attacking Abyssinia. The Nazis began to persecute Germany's Jews even more harshly. Most people felt that war was inevitable.

THE MUNICH AGREEMENT

On 30 September 1938, the British and French governments signed an agreement in Munich, allowing Hitler to take over part of Czechoslovakia. Chamberlain (left), the British prime minister, flew home with Hitler's signature on a peace deal. While many people felt relieved, others were not convinced. Their doubts were proved right. In 1939 Hitler occupied the rest of Czechoslovakia. Then he made a "no-war" treaty with Stalin, leader of the USSR, and they agreed to share Poland.

WAR BEGINS IN EUROPE, 1939

Hitler sent his armies into Poland on 1 September 1939. World War II had begun. The Poles asked for help from their allies, Britain and France. On 3 September, Britain and France declared war on Germany. Neither country did much to help Poland, which was occupied by German and Soviet armies. In 1940, Hitler invaded France, and by the end of the year, the Nazis occupied most of western Europe.

❝ I have nothing to offer but blood, toil, tears, and sweat. ❞
Winston Churchill, 13 May 1940

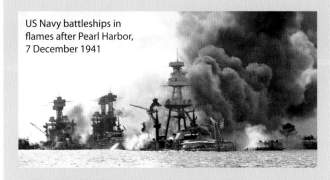

US Navy battleships in flames after Pearl Harbor, 7 December 1941

THE WORLD AT WAR, 1941

For a time, only Britain and its Commonwealth allies, such as Australia and Canada, stood against the Nazis. The US government sent aid to Britain, but did not join the war. However, in 1941, Hitler attacked the USSR, and later that year Japan attacked the US at Pearl Harbor in Hawaii. Now the war was a global conflict, stretching from Europe to the Pacific. It would be the most destructive war in history, and shape the world as we know it today.

WORLD WAR II TIMELINE

World War II lasted six years, from September 1939 to August 1945. Every year of the war brought changes in fortunes for the warring nations: victories and defeats, setback and triumphs. For many people who lived, and fought, through the war years, these were the most important days of their lives, dates they never forgot.

1941

7 DECEMBER
Japan attacks the US naval base of Pearl Harbor, Hawaii

6 APRIL
Axis forces attack Greece and Yugoslavia

8 DECEMBER
US and Britain declare war on Japan

8 SEPTEMBER
German armies attack city of Leningrad in Soviet Union

22 JUNE
German armies invade the Soviet Union

1942

15 FEBRUARY
Japanese capture Singapore, after invading Malaya

9 APRIL
US and Philippine forces surrender to Japan at Bataan

7 AUGUST
US Marines land on Guadalcanal

11 NOVEMBER
British win Battle of El Alamein in North Africa

26 FEBRUARY
Japanese navy wins battle in the Java Sea

8 MAY
Allies win naval battle in the Coral Sea

6 JUNE
Allies defeat Japanese at the Battle of Midway

23 AUGUST
German armies attack Stalingrad in Soviet Union

1945

9 AUGUST
Allies drop second atomic bomb on Nagasaki, Japan

6 AUGUST
Allies drop an atomic bomb on Hiroshima, Japan

"LET US GO FORWARD TOGETHER"

7 MAY
Germany surrenders

2 SEPTEMBER
Japan surrenders, ending World War II

8 AUGUST
Soviets declare war on Japan

In dark times, posters encouraged people to be hopeful

8 MAY
VE (Victory in Europe) Day

30 APRIL
Hitler kills himself after Soviets enter Berlin

1939

1 SEPTEMBER
Germany invades Poland

3 SEPTEMBER
Britain and France at
war with Germany

**Hitler's armies
advanced across
Europe in a series of
lightning military
campaigns**

1940

10 JULY – 31 OCTOBER: Battle of Britain

7 SEPTEMBER
Start of the Blitz –
air raids on Britain

10 JUNE
Italy declares war on
France and Britain

10 MAY
Germany invades Belgium,
Netherlands, and France.
Churchill is now British
prime minister.

9 APRIL
Germany invades
Denmark and Norway

22 JUNE
France signs a ceasefire
with Germany

1943

JANUARY
US bombers raid
Germany from Britain

13 MAY
Axis troops in North
Africa surrender to Allies

9 SEPTEMBER
Allies land at Salerno
in southern Italy

2 FEBRUARY
German troops
surrender at Stalingrad

10 JULY
Allied forces
land in Sicily

JULY
Battle of Kursk
in Soviet Union

20 NOVEMBER
US forces land on
Pacific island of Tarawa

1944

20 OCTOBER
Allies begin
liberation of the
Philippines

19 JUNE
US naval victory
over Japan in
Battle of the
Philippine Sea

6 JUNE
D-Day: Allied armies land
in Normandy (France)

13 JUNE
V-1 flying bombs hit
southern England

26 OCTOBER
Allies win Battle
of Leyte Gulf over
Japanese navy

20 JUNE
German generals'
plot to kill Hitler fails

**The Allied
landings
in Normandy
marked a turning
point in the war**

THE WAR IN EUROPE, NORTH AFRICA, AND THE MEDITERRANEAN

In the first years of World War II, from 1939 to 1942, Axis forces were on the attack. They occupied much of Europe, and invaded North Africa. In 1941, they invaded the USSR. The Allies hit back by air bombing, and won a key battle at El Alamein, in Egypt. By 1943 the tide was turning, as the Allies landed first in North Africa and then in Italy, and Soviet armies pushed back the Germans. In Italy, Mussolini fell from power. In 1944 the Allies in the west began the liberation of France with the D-Day landings in Normandy, while in the east, Soviet armies advanced towards Germany. The war ended with the invasion of Germany and the fall of Berlin in May 1945.

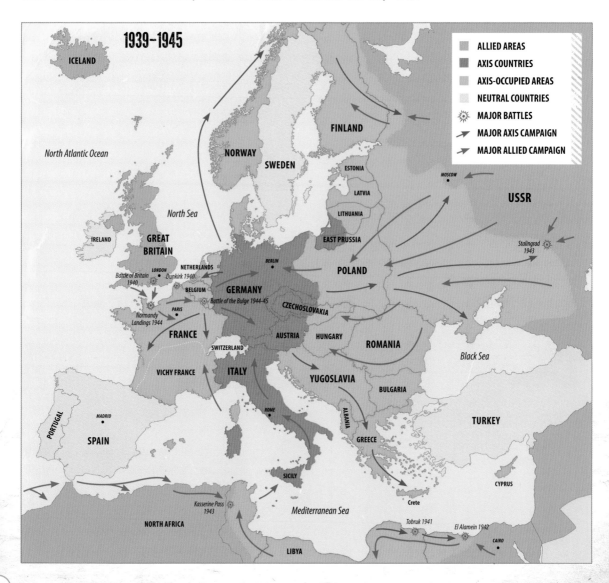

1939–1945

	ALLIED AREAS
	AXIS COUNTRIES
	AXIS-OCCUPIED AREAS
	NEUTRAL COUNTRIES
	MAJOR BATTLES
	MAJOR AXIS CAMPAIGN
	MAJOR ALLIED CAMPAIGN

ICELAND

North Atlantic Ocean

NORWAY

SWEDEN

FINLAND

ESTONIA

LATVIA

LITHUANIA

MOSCOW

USSR

North Sea

IRELAND

GREAT BRITAIN

EAST PRUSSIA

Stalingrad 1943

LONDON

NETHERLANDS

BERLIN

Dunkirk 1940

POLAND

Battle of Britain 1940

BELGIUM

GERMANY

Battle of the Bulge 1944-45

CZECHOSLOVAKIA

PARIS

Normandy Landings 1944

FRANCE

SWITZERLAND

AUSTRIA

HUNGARY

ROMANIA

Black Sea

VICHY FRANCE

ITALY

YUGOSLAVIA

BULGARIA

PORTUGAL

MADRID

ROME

ALBANIA

TURKEY

SPAIN

GREECE

CYPRUS

SICILY

Crete

Kasserine Pass 1943

Mediterranean Sea

Tobruk 1941

El Alamein 1942

CAIRO

NORTH AFRICA

LIBYA

THE WAR IN THE PACIFIC AND ASIA

Japan was already at war in China when its forces attacked the US at Pearl Harbor in 1941, bringing the US into World War II. Japanese armies and naval forces swiftly overran much of southeast Asia, including Malaya and Singapore. There was fighting in Burma and in the Philippines, threatening both India and Australia. Japan's victories were halted by the Allies in 1942, and the Allies fought their way from island to island, and through southeast Asia. Many key battles were fought at sea and in the jungles, but it was airpower and the atomic bombs on Hiroshima and Nagasaki that brought World War II to its close in August 1945.

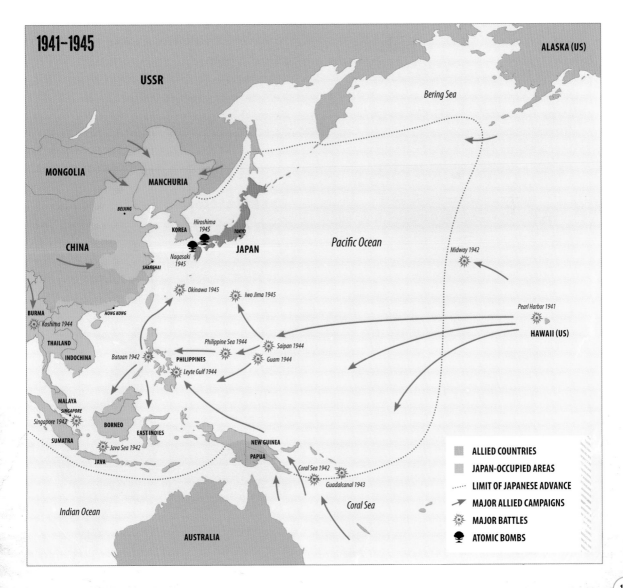

1941–1945

ALASKA (US)

USSR

Bering Sea

MONGOLIA

MANCHURIA

BEIJING

Hiroshima 1945

KOREA

TOKYO

Pacific Ocean

Midway 1942

CHINA

Nagasaki 1945

JAPAN

SHANGHAI

Okinawa 1945

Iwo Jima 1945

Pearl Harbor 1941

BURMA

HONG KONG

Koshima 1944

HAWAII (US)

THAILAND

Philippine Sea 1944

Saipan 1944

INDOCHINA

Bataan 1942

PHILIPPINES

Guam 1944

Leyte Gulf 1944

MALAYA

SINGAPORE

Singapore 1942

BORNEO

EAST INDIES

SUMATRA

Java Sea 1942

NEW GUINEA

JAVA

PAPUA

Coral Sea 1942

Guadalcanal 1943

Indian Ocean

Coral Sea

AUSTRALIA

ALLIED COUNTRIES
JAPAN-OCCUPIED AREAS
LIMIT OF JAPANESE ADVANCE
MAJOR ALLIED CAMPAIGNS
MAJOR BATTLES
ATOMIC BOMBS

FACTS AND FIGURES

There were 4,066 landing craft in the Allied invasion fleet on D-Day (6 June 1944).

The heaviest WWII bomb was the RAF's "Grand Slam" at 9,975 kg (22,000 lb).

The greatest loss of life was in the Soviet Union, where at least 22 million people died.

In January 1945, the overloaded German refugee ship Wilhelm Gustloff was sunk by a Russian submarine. It was the worst ever maritime disaster - more than 9,000 people died.

The B-24 Liberator bomber had 1.5 million parts.

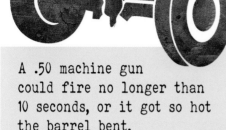

The 1944 US "Stratosphere" anti-aircraft gun could shoot a shell 17.7 km (11 miles) high.

A .50 machine gun could fire no longer than 10 seconds, or it got so hot the barrel bent.

The biggest air force was the USAAF. In July 1944 it had nearly 80,000 aircraft.

World War II cost more in material damage than all other wars in history put together.

The biggest wartime convoy was 167 ships in 1944.

The heaviest tank was the German Maus II. It weighed 195 tonnes, but never went into battle.

The biggest submarines were the Japanese I-14, I-40, and I-400. They were 122 m (400 ft) long and each carried three seaplanes.

The greatest airborne landing was at Arnhem, Netherlands, in September 1944, with 2,800 aircraft and 1,800 gliders.

Japanese troops used elephants to pull trucks out of mud.

The Channel Islands, occupied by the Nazis in 1940, were the only part of the British Isles to be captured.

The siege of Leningrad lasted 880 days (30 August 1941 to 27 January 1944), the longest siege in history.

In 1940, it took about 20,000 anti-aircraft shells to shoot down one bomber plane.

The biggest naval battle ever was at Leyte Gulf (22-27 October 1944) in the Pacific, with 166 Allied and 75 Japanese ships, and more than 2,000 aircraft.

AFTER THE WAR

The war left a legacy of destruction. The exact number of people who died will never be known, but most estimates put the figure at more than 55 million. Almost two-thirds of those who died were civilians. Some nations bore a particularly high cost – the USSR and China both lost tens of millions, while Poland lost 16 per cent of its population.

MILITARY DEATHS DURING WORLD WAR II

- OTHERS 1,422,500
- SOVIET UNION 10,700,000
- JAPAN 2,120,000
- ITALY 301,400
- GERMANY 5,533,000
- FRANCE 217,600
- POLAND 160,000
- CHINA 3,800,000
- BRITAIN AND COMMONWEALTH 575,000
- UNITED STATES 416,800

CIVILIAN WAR DEATHS 1937-1945

- OTHERS 8,450,600
- SOVIET UNION 12,400,000
- JAPAN 1,000,000
- ITALY 153,100
- GERMANY 1,760,000
- FRANCE 350,000
- POLAND 5,440,000
- CHINA 16,200,000
- BRITAIN AND COMMONWEALTH 1,568,500

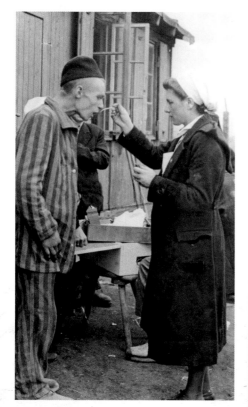

A nurse tends to a liberated concentration camp survivor, 1945

WAR DAMAGE

Bombing and battles destroyed many cities, especially in Germany (below) and Japan. Germany was left divided. Japan was under Allied control. More than 12 million people in Europe were homeless. Some had survived the concentration camps, others had fled homelands and could not return. To rebuild war damage, the Allies set up schemes such as Marshall Aid (1948). Courts were set up to try Nazis and Japanese leaders for war crimes.

REBUILDING

Soldiers came home to their old jobs, and factories went back to making cars and furniture instead of tanks and planes. New buildings were built on blitzed "bomb sites". Shattered cities like Berlin, Tokyo, Warsaw, and Dresden would be slowly rebuilt. The United Nations was set up in 1945 to try and ensure world peace in the future.

TENSIONS AND COLD WAR

World War II left Britain and France weaker than before. Their overseas empires broke up as India, Vietnam, and other colonies sought independence. Wartime Allies did not stay friends. The United States opposed the Soviet Union, which forced Communism on eastern Europe. By 1949, China was a Communist power, and the USSR had its own atomic bomb. In a new "Cold War", the USA and USSR confronted one another, with even more terrifying weapons.

SHAPING THE FUTURE

It took many years for the scars of World War II to heal. The Holocaust, and the atomic bombs at Hiroshima and Nagasaki, were warnings for all humanity. Many Jews left Europe for Israel. France and Germany became partners with other nations in what is now the European Union. Japan prospered as a democracy, while China grew to be a superpower. The USSR broke apart by the 1990s, bringing the Cold War to an end. Many of these changes were the direct results of World War II – a war that had shaken the world.

GLOSSARY

AA gun
Anti-aircraft gun, for shooting at planes.

Admiral
Highest rank in the navy.

Afrika Korps
The German army in North Africa.

Air raid
Attack by aircraft dropping bombs.

Aircraft carrier
Warship with flight deck ("flat-top") for aircraft.

Allies
The nations fighting against the Axis powers, including Britain, the US, and the USSR - a total of 50 countries by 1945.

Amphibious
Describes a vehicle able to travel on water and land.

Atomic bomb
A very powerful type of bomb that releases the energy in atoms to create a massive explosion.

Axis powers
The nations fighting against the Allies, chiefly Germany, Italy, and Japan.

Battalion
A large military unit that is ready for battle, made up of companies.

Battleship
Very large warship with big guns.

Bayonet
A stabbing knife fitted to the barrel of a rifle.

Bazooka
Hand-held weapon that fires an explosive missile.

The Blitz
German air raids on British cities that began in 1940 and ended in 1941.

Blitzkrieg
German for "lightning war", the tactics of massed ground and air attacks used by the Nazis to win fast victories.

Bomber
Aircraft designed to drop bombs.

Burma Road
Route from India to China, closed by Japan in 1942.

Camouflage
Disguise, such as mottled paint or clothing.

Carbine
Rifle with a short barrel.

Casualties
People injured or killed.

Civil defence
Protecting civilians from attack, especially from the air.

Civilian
A person who is not in the armed forces.

Column
A long line of soldiers and vehicles.

Commandos
Soldiers who are specially trained to carry out surprise attacks and raids.

Commonwealth
Countries formerly part of the British Empire.

Communism
Political system based on state ownership. The USSR was governed by the Communist Party.

Company
The smallest subdivision of a battalion.

Concentration camp
A Nazi prison camp.

Conscription
Compulsory military service.

Convoy
Ships or trucks moving in a group.

Corvette
Small warship used to hunt submarines.

Cruiser
A warship that is smaller than a battleship, but similarly armed.

D-Day
Code-name for 6 June 1944, the Allied invasion of Normandy, France.

Depth charge
Underwater bomb dropped from a ship to damage a submarine.

Destroyer
Small warship used in many roles.

Dive-bomber
Plane that attacks in a steep dive to drop a bomb.

Division
Army unit with about 15,000 soldiers, plus guns and vehicles.

DUKW
Amphibious truck that could travel on land or water, first used in 1943.

Enigma
German machine for encoding secret messages.

Enola Gay
B-29 bomber that dropped the first atomic bomb.

Evacuees
Children and adults who were evacuated, moved from danger to safer places.

Fascism
Political system in Italy from the 1920s and Germany from the 1930s.

Field marshal
Highest army rank in British and German armies.

Fighter
Fast aircraft for attacking enemy planes.

Fighter-bomber
Fighter that has been modified to carry bombs.

Fire-bomb
An incendiary bomb that bursts into flames on impact.

Firestorm
Fire that sucks in surrounding air.

Flak
Anti-aircraft fire from the German Flugzeugabwehrkanone ("aircraft attack gun").

Flying boat
Aircraft able to land and take off on water.

Free French
French forces in exile after 1940, led by Charles de Gaulle.

Front
Battle zone where opposing forces face one another.

General
Commander of an army; highest rank in US army.

Gestapo
Short for Geheime Staatspolizei, the Nazi secret police.

Ghetto
An area of a city where Jews were forced by the Nazis to live.

GI
"General Issue", a term for an American soldier.

Glider
Towed troop-carrying aircraft.

Grenade
A small bomb thrown or fired from a rifle.

Guerrilla war
A war fought by people who are not part of the regular armed forces and who use tactics such as sabotage and ambush.

Holocaust
The mass murder of Jews and other minorities by the Nazis, from 1941 to 1945.

Howitzer
Artillery gun that fires shells high in the air.

Incendiary
A device that causes fires; a fire-bomb.

Infantry
Soldiers that fight mostly on foot.

Intelligence
Information learned about the enemy.

Jeep
Small, four-wheeled army vehicle.

Jet plane
Aircraft with turbojet thrust engine, instead of a piston engine turning a propeller.

Jew
Person who follows the religion of Judaism.

Kamikaze
Japanese suicide pilot.

Landing craft
Open, flat-bottomed craft for beach landings.

Luftwaffe
The German air force.

Machine gun
Quick-firing gun used by armies, ships, and aircraft.

Magazine
Snap-in holder containing bullets, for loading a gun.

Maginot Line
A system of French fortifications along the French-German border, 1939.

Manhattan Project
Secret effort by the Allies to make the first atomic bombs.

Maquis
The Resistance in Nazi-occupied France.

Marines
Soldiers trained to land from ships. The US Marine Corps also had its own planes.

Mine
An explosive device that detonates when struck.

Mortar
Small artillery weapon.

NATO
North Atlantic Treaty Organization, an association set up in 1949 for the defence of Europe and the North Atlantic.

Nazis
Members of the National Socialist German Workers party, led by Adolf Hitler, which ruled Germany from 1933 to 1945.

Neutral
A country not involved in the war, such as Ireland or Sweden.

Night-fighter
Aircraft adapted to hunt bombers in darkness.

Nuremberg
German city in which war crimes trials were held after the war.

Occupation
Sending in armed forces to control all, or part, of another country.

OSS
Office of Strategic Services, US agency for spies and sabotage.

Panzers
German tanks and other armoured vehicles.

Paratroops
Soldiers who dropped from planes by parachute.

Partisan
A Resistance fighter.

Pathfinders
Aircraft that led bombing raids.

Pearl Harbor
US naval base in Hawaii, attacked by Japan in December 1941.

Phoney War
Name given to the period from November 1939 to April 1940 when there were no major battles.

Platoon
Small group of soldiers, often 20 or so.

Poison gas
Chemical weapons, not used in battle, but used to kill victims in Nazi death camps.

POW
Short for "prisoner of war", a person captured in combat.

Propaganda
Information and "misinformation" (such as radio, film, leaflets) distributed to boost your own side and demoralize or mislead the enemy.

PT boat
Small, fast motor boat.

Radar
Use of radio waves to detect aircraft, invented in the 1930s.

RAF
Britain's Royal Air Force.

Range
How far a gun can fire or a plane can fly.

Rations
Food and other provisions that soldiers took with them into combat.

Reconnaissance
Gathering information about enemy activity.

Red Army
The army of the USSR, made up of about 12 million men and women in WWII.

Refugee
Homeless person fleeing in search of safety.

Regiment
Army unit made up of battalions and companies.

Resistance
Fighters opposing an enemy who has occupied their country.

Rifle
Soldier's usual weapon, a long-barrelled firearm.

Sabotage
Deliberate damage to equipment or transport links - for example, by wrecking a factory or blowing up railway tracks.

Searchlight
Powerful light used to spot enemy bombers at night.

Sniper
Marksman with a rifle, shooting from a distance.

Snorkel
Long air-tube in a submarine, which sucks in air so the sub can operate while submerged.

SOE
Special Operations Executive, a British organization that sent secret agents into Nazi-occupied territory.

Sonar
Sound-echo device for detecting and hunting submarines.

Special forces
Troops trained for secret missions and raids.

SS
German Schutzstaffel ("protection squad"), the Nazi private army set up as Hitler's bodyguard, which later managed concentration camps. The Waffen ("fighting") SS were elite soldiers.

Tank
Armoured land vehicle with a large cannon.

Third Reich
Name for Germany under Nazi rule.

Torpedo
Powered projectile that travels underwater to blow up ships.

Tracer
A bullet that glows to show its flightpath.

Turret
Movable part of a tank, ship, or plane, fitted with guns.

U-boat
Short for Unterseeboot ("undersea boat"), a German submarine.

Ultra
German secrets read by Allied code-breakers.

United Nations
International peace-keeping organization set up in 1945.

USAAF
The US air force.

USSR
Short for Union of Soviet Socialist Republics - of which Russia was part; also known as the Soviet Union.

V-1
German pilotless flying bomb, first used in 1944.

V-2
German rocket missile, first fired against England in 1944.

Vichy France
Part of southern France that was not occupied by the Nazis in 1940, governed by Marshal Philippe Pétain.

Victoria Cross
Medal for bravery, the highest award for members of the British and Commonwealth armed forces.

INDEX

ACKNOWLEDGEMENTS

The publisher would like to thank the following for their kind permission to reproduce their photographs:

(Key: a-above; b-below/bottom; c-centre; f-far; l-left; r-right; t-top)

1 Dreamstime.com: (t). 3 Corbis: Bettmann (bc); Hulton-Deutsch Collection (br). 4 Corbis: (bl). 5 Dorling Kindersley: The Old Flying Machine Company (tr). Imperial War Museum: (bl). 6 Corbis: Swim Ink 2, LLC (c). 8 Corbis: Swim Ink 2, LLC (c). 9 Corbis: The Print Collector. 10 Corbis: Swim Ink (c). 11 Corbis: Bettmann (c). 12 Bridgeman Images: Private Collection (l). 13 Alamy Images: Time Magazine Cover 21 May 1945, Uber Bilder (r). 14 Getty Images: The LIFE Picture Collection (c). 15 Getty Images: Print Collector (c). 16 Corbis: (c). 17 Corbis: Oscar White (c). 18 Corbis: Swim Ink 2, LLC (c). 19 Corbis. 20 Corbis: Bettmann (br). 21 Corbis: Hulton-Deutsch Collection (c). 22 Corbis: Kingendai / AFLO (c). 23 Corbis: Bettmann (r). 24 Corbis: Hulton-Deutsch Collection (c). 25 Alamy Images: Universal Art Archive (r). RAF Battle of Britain Memorial Flight: (c). 26 Alamy Images: Interfoto (l). 27 Getty Images: Roger Viollet (c). 28 Corbis: Oscar White (c). 29 Library and Archives Canada: (r). 30 Corbis: Swim Ink 2, LLC (c). 31 Corbis: Hulton-Deutsch Collection (br). 32 Imperial War Museum: (c). 33 AF Eisenbahn Archiv: Private Collection. 34 Corbis: Bettmann (c). 35 Getty Images: Popperfoto (cl). 36 Rex Features: Associated Newspapers / Daily (cl). 37 Getty Images: ITAR-TASS / Sovfoto (c). 38 Corbis: Bettmann (c). 39 Getty Images: Gamma-Keystone via Getty Images (c). 40 Getty Images: (c). 41 Getty Images: 100% Keystone (c). 42 Mirrorpix: (l). 43 Getty Images: (c). 44 Corbis: Swim Ink 2, LLC (c). 45 Getty Images: (c). 46 Rex Features: Stuart Clarke / Mail On Sunday (c). 47 Alamy Images: Universal Art Archive (c). 48 Getty Images: (c). 49 Imperial War Museum: (c). 50 Corbis: Swim Ink 2, LLC (c). 51 Rex Features: East News (r). 52 Alamy Images: AF Fotografie (l). 53 Getty Images: The LIFE Picture Collection (c). 54 Dreamstime.com: Imaengine (r). 55 Getty Images: Heritage Images (c). 56 Corbis: Swim Ink 2, LLC (c). 58 Malcolm McGregor: (c). 59 Malcolm McGregor: (c). 60 Malcolm McGregor: (c). 61 Malcolm McGregor: (c). 62 Malcolm McGregor: (c). 63 Malcolm McGregor: (c). 64 Malcolm McGregor: (c). 65 Malcolm McGregor: (c). 66 Malcolm McGregor: (c). 67 Malcolm McGregor: (c). 68 Malcolm McGregor: (c). 69 Malcolm McGregor: (c). 70 Malcolm McGregor: (c). 71 Malcolm McGregor. 72 Malcolm McGregor: (c). 73 Malcolm McGregor: (c). 74 Malcolm McGregor. 75 Malcolm McGregor: (c). 76 Malcolm McGregor: (c). 77 Malcolm McGregor: (c). 78 Malcolm McGregor: (c). 79 Malcolm McGregor: (c). 80 Corbis: Heritage Images (c). 82 Corbis: Heritage Images (c). 83 Corbis: Bettmann (c). 84 Corbis: Hulton-Deutsch Collection (c). 85 Alamy Images: Universal Art Archive (b). 86 Corbis: picture alliance (c). 87 Getty Images: UIG via Getty Images (c). 88 Dorling Kindersley: The Tank Museum (cl); Royal Museum of the Armed Forces and of Military History, Brussels, Belgium (cr). 88-89 Getty Images: UIG via Getty Images (c). 90 Corbis: Hulton-Deutsch Collection (bc). 90-91 Corbis: Bettmann (c). 92-93 Corbis: (c) 93 Corbis: (tr). 94 Corbis: Hulton-Deutsch Collection (c). 95 Corbis: Consolidated US Army / dpa (c). 96 Corbis: Hulton-Deutsch Collection (c). 97 Corbis: Bettmann (c). 98 Corbis: (c). 99 Corbis: Hulton-Deutsch Collection (c). 100 Corbis: The Dmitri Baltermants Collection (c). 102 Corbis: Heritage Images (c). 103 Corbis: Michael Nicholson (c). 104 Getty Images: (c). 105 Corbis: (c). 106 Corbis: Heritage Images (c). 107 Corbis: Hulton-Deutsch Collection (c). 108 Getty Images: (c). 109 akg-images: ullstein bild. 110 Corbis: (c). 111 Imperial War Museum: (c). 112 Corbis: (c). 113 Corbis: Bettmann (c). 114-115 Getty Images: The LIFE Picture Collection (c). 115 Getty Images: The LIFE Picture Collection (tr). 116 Corbis: Hulton-Deutsch Collection (c). 117 Getty Images: (c). 118 Corbis: Heritage Images (c). 119 Corbis: Bettmann (c). 120-121 Corbis: (c). 121 Corbis: (tr). 122 Getty Images: SSPL / Planet News Archive (c). 123 Corbis: Bettmann (c). 124 Getty Images: Keystone (b). 125 Corbis: (c). 126 Corbis: (c). 127 Corbis: Bettmann (c). 128 Corbis: (c). 129 Corbis: Horace Bristol (c). 130 Corbis: Bettmann (c). 131 Corbis: (c). 132 Corbis: SuperStock (c). 133 Corbis: (c). 134-135 Corbis: National Geographic Society (c). 136 Corbis: National Geographic Society (c). 137 Dreamstime.com: Sergei Butorin. 138 Alamy Images: Martin Bennett (c). 139 Corbis: Hulton-Deutsch Collection (c). 141 Dorling Kindersley: The Tank Museum (c). 142 Corbis: Michael Kappeler / dpa (c). 143 Imperial War Museum: (c). 144 Corbis: National Geographic Society (c). 145 Corbis: Bettmann (c). 146 Dorling Kindersley: RAF Battle of Britain Memorial Flight (c). 147 Corbis: Bettmann (c). 148 Dorling Kindersley: Planes of Fame Air Museum, Chino, California (c). 149 Dorling Kindersley: The Old Flying Machine Company (c). 153 Dorling Kindersley: Aces High Limited, Hangar 6 (c). 155 Corbis: Museum of Flight (c). 156 Corbis: ClassicStock (c). 157 Corbis: Bettmann (c). 158 Getty Images: UIG via Getty Images (c). 160 Corbis: National Geographic Society. 161 Corbis: Hulton-Deutsch Collection (c). 162 Alamy Images: Universal Art Archive (b). 163 Corbis: (c). 165 Dorling Kindersley: Scale Model World (c). 166 Imperial War Museum: (c). 167 Courtesy of U.S. Navy: NH 68912. 169 Corbis: Bettmann (c). 170 Corbis: National Geographic Society (c). 171 Dorling Kindersley: Gary Ombler (c). 172 Corbis: Berliner Verlag / Archiv / dpa (c). 173 Getty Images: (c). 174 Getty Images: UIG via Getty Images (c). 175 Lebrecht Music and Arts: Sueddeutsche Zeitung Photo. 176 Corbis: National Geographic Society (c). 177 Dorling Kindersley: Gatwick Aviation Museum (c). 178 Corbis: Bettmann (c). 179 Corbis: (c). 180 Getty Images: SSPL / Bletchley Park Trust (c). 182 Getty Images: (c). 183 Alamy Images: Berliner (bl). Anatoly Zak: RussianSpaceWeb.com (c). 185 Dorling Kindersley: Gatwick Aviation Museum (c). 186 Corbis: Bettmann (c). 187 Mary Evans Picture Library: Hugh W. Cowin Aviation Collection (c). 189 Corbis: (c). 192 Corbis: (c). 193 Corbis: (cr); Hulton-Deutsch Collection (tl). 194 Corbis: David Pollack (bc). 195 Corbis: (tr); Hulton-Deutsch Collection (br). 200 Corbis: Bettmann (br); dpa / dpa (bl). 201 Corbis: English Heritage / Arcaid (tc); John Swope Collection (br).

All other images © Dorling Kindersley
For further information see:

www.dkimages.com